I0813849

# THE LONDON ENVIRO 400 MMC AND CITY

# THE LONDON ENVIRO 400 MMC AND CITY

DAVID BEDDALL

First published in Great Britain in 2025 by
Pen and Sword Transport
An imprint of
Pen & Sword Books Ltd.
Yorkshire - Philadelphia



ISBN 978 1 03610 961 5



A CIP catalogue record for this book is available from the British Library.



Typeset by SJmagic DESIGN SERVICES, India.

The Publisher's authorised representative in the EU for product safety is Authorised Rep Compliance Ltd., Ground Floor, 71 Lower Baggot Street, Dublin D02 P593, Ireland.
www.arccompliance.com

For a complete list of Pen & Sword titles please contact

PEN & SWORD BOOKS LIMITED
George House, Beevor Street, Off Pontefract Road, Hoyle Mill, Barnsley,
South Yorkshire, England, S71 1HN.
E-mail: enquiries@pen-and-sword.co.uk
Website: www.pen-and-sword.co.uk

or

PEN AND SWORD BOOKS
1950 Lawrence Rd, Havertown, PA 19083, USA
E-mail: uspen-and-sword@casematepublishers.com
Website: www.penandswordbooks.com

# CONTENTS

# ACKNOWLEDGEMENTS

I would like to thank my family for their continued support during the production of this book, to my mum and dad for always being there and supporting me. To my wife Helen for putting up with the countless conversations about the various aspects of the book. My thanks also go to my nephew Liam Farrer-Beddall for once again allowing me to use photographs from his collection, and for making special trips to London to get certain photographs that I have requested. All photographs, unless stated otherwise, were taken by Liam Farrer-Beddall. I would also like to thank Ben Everitt and Rob Waughman for allowing me to use their photographs in this book.

# INTRODUCTION

The Enviro 400 MMC (Major Model Change) was introduced on 1 May 2014 by Alexander Dennis Limited, with the first examples arriving in London during 2015. As the MMC part of the title suggests, the appearance of the body design was completely changed. Originally built alongside the Enviro 400, the MMC replaced the standard model in 2018. After this time, the original Enviro 400 became known as the 'classic' model. Since its introduction, many operators around the United Kingdom have taken stock of the Enviro 400 MMC, with Stagecoach being the largest customer. Other major operating groups in the UK have also taken significant numbers of the type including Go-Ahead, National Express, First and Arriva. Transdev and Yellow Buses also took a small number of the type into stock along with some independent operators. A tri-axle version of the Enviro 400 MMC was launched in 2018, this becoming known as the Enviro 400 XLB. No orders for London operators were received, with a number operating with Lothian Buses, and a smaller fleet operating with Stagecoach East on the Cambridgeshire Busway.

The Enviro 400 Virtual Electric was introduced in 2015, this not being successful and only five were manufactured, three of which entered service with Tower Transit in London.

A new style of Enviro 400 was also launched in 2015, this being named the Enviro 400 City. This model took features from both the Enviro 200 MMC and the New Bus for London. It featured glass where the staircase was, and a curved top-deck rear end similar to that featured on the Enviro 200 MMC. Whilst the diesel and hybrid versions of this type were not purchased in large quantities, the Enviro 400 City came into its own when it was mounted on the BYD D8UR DD electric chassis.

The Enviro 400 MMC body was not exclusively mounted on the AD E40D or E40H model. Orders also saw the Enviro 400 MMC placed on the Volvo B5TL and B5LH models, with the latter type being operated by London operators. In 2019 the Scania N250UD became another option, but none were operated in London.

London's Enviro 400 MMC and Enviro 400 City details the various Enviro 400 MMC and Enviro 400 City / Enviro 400EV City buses that are operated by London operators, the information being up to date as of September 2024.

David Beddall
Rushden, September 2024

# DEMONSTRATOR

**YY64GXG was** the London demonstrator for the Enviro 400 MMC. It is photographed in Brixton on its way to the Old Kent Road Tesco terminus of route 415 whilst operating with Abellio London.

An unregistered AD Enviro 400 MMC bodied AD E40D double-deck was displayed at the Abellio London Walworth garage open day in July 2014. The vehicle concerned was registered YY64GXG in November and was demonstrated at this time around various National Express West Midlands garages.

It returned to London in December 2014, being allocated to Abellio London. It was allocated to Beddington where it was used on driver familiarisation work ahead of the introduction of a batch of Enviro 400 MMCs for route 109. It transferred within Abellio to Walworth in January 2015, again being used for driver familiarisation work. A month later it was also used on peak services on the 381. Numbered 2400 by Abellio, it entered service in February. It was retained by Abellio London until December 2016, at which time it moved on to CT Plus. It was used to replace Enviro 400 City 2510, this bus being damaged by fire in October. It entered service in January 2017 on the 26.

# ABELLIO LONDON/ TRANSPORT UK

The first Enviro 400 MMCs entered the Abellio London fleet at the end of 2014. 2487 to 2498 (YY64TYD/F/G/H/K/O/P/S/T/U/V/W) all arrived during December. These were of the E40H hybrid model and were allocated to Beddington for use on the 109. As mentioned in the previous chapter, the ADL demonstrator YY64GXG was loaned at this time to assist Abellio with driver familiarisation work. They were joined at Beddington in January 2015 by 2499 to 2513 (YY64TYX/Z, TZA-H/J-N), also for use on the 109 (Croydon, Park Street–Brixton Station).

A second batch of Enviro 400 MMCs arrived in January, these being for the 415 (Tulse Hill Station–Old Kent Road Tesco), the route being extended from Elephant & Castle to Old Kent Road at the time of takeover. It followed on as 2514 and carried registration mark YY64TZO. It was added to Walworth's allocation. The full allocation arrived in March. These continued the numbering sequence on from 2515 to 2522. Registration marks YX15OWD/E/F/G/H/J/K/N were allocated to these eight double-deckers. Some of these were delivered to Abellio after they took over the 415 from Arriva London South on 7 March. 2516 and 2517 swapped identities in April after they entered service with incorrect registration marks. 2516 originally carried YX15OWE, becoming YX15OWF, with 2517 originally carrying YX15OWF, this being altered to YX15OWE. However, in June 2015 these two buses were renumbered, with 2516 (YX15OWF) being renumbered 2517, and 2517 (YX15OWE) taking up stock number 2516.

Six additional Enviro 400 MMC bodied E40Hs arrived in March, this time finding a home at Abellio's Hayes garage. 2523 to 2528 (YX15OWO/P/R/U/V/W) were put to use on the 350 (Hayes & Harlington Station–Heathrow Terminal 5). 2529 to 2531 (YX15OWY/Z, OXA) completed delivery when they arrived in April.

To cover the extension of the 415, two additional Enviro 400 MMCs were delivered to Abellio in July. These took up registration marks YX15OXB and YX15OXC, and followed on from those used on the 350, becoming 2532 and 2533 respectively, these joining the others at Walworth.

Just over a year passed before further Enviro 400 MMCs arrived with Abellio. Eighteen E40Hs were taken into stock at Battersea during August 2016 to update the rolling stock on the 344 (Clapham Junction–Liverpool Street). These were numbered 2534 to 2551 which were allocated registration marks YY16YKA-G, YKM/K/L/H/J, YKN/O/P/R/S/T.

**2496 (YY64TYU)** was delivered to Abellio London in December 2014 for use on the 109. It is seen passing through Streatham High Street shortly after arrival.

**March 2015** saw the majority of the fleet of Enviro 400 MMCs for route 415 taken into stock by Abellio. The last member of the batch, 2522 (YX15OWM), is seen passing Brixton Police Station on its way to Tulse Hill Station.

**The third** consignment of Enviro 400 MMCs to operate with Abellio London were allocated to their West London garage in Hayes. 2530 (YX15OWZ) is photographed in Hayes and Harlington after just starting its journey to Heathrow Terminal 5.

**The 415** was extended in March 2015 which required two extra buses. The second member of the pair, 2533, YX15OXC, is found negotiating Elephant & Castle.

In 2017, twenty-five Enviro 400 MMCs arrived for use on the 427 (Uxbridge–Acton Town Hall), this being taken over from Metroline. Allocated to Hayes these buses took up stock numbers 2552 to 2576 (YX17NUW/Y, NVA-H/J-P/R-W/Y/Z). 2552-64 put in an appearance in March, with 2565-76 following in April.

2017 also saw a swap in allocation between the 350 and U5. The Enviro 400 MMCs from the 350 (2523-31) were swapped onto the U5. This required three additional buses, these being covered by the arrival of 2577 to 2579 (YX17NPP/U/V). These were allocated to Fulwell in July, with the 2523-31 moving to Fulwell in March. These buses transferred from Fulwell back to Hayes in August 2017 along with the U5.

An order for forty-one Enviro 400 MMCs was placed during 2017 to cover the take up of routes 45 (Clapham Park–King's Cross) and 196 (Elephant & Castle–Norwood Junction) from Go-Ahead London. 2580 to 2602 (YY67GZA-H/J-P/R-X/Z) arrived ahead of the takeover of route 45 on 11 November. Arriving in October, these were initially placed into store at Beddington before moving to Walworth.

Those intended for use on the 196 were delivered to Abellio in April 2018. These were again allocated to Walworth. Registrations SN18KKR/S/U/V/W/X/Y/Z, KLA/C/D/E/F/J/K/L were carried by these buses which followed on from those used on the 45, taking up rolling stock numbers 2603 to 2618.

A shift was made in 2019 from the E40H hybrid model to the newly introduced E40D smart hybrid Enviro 400 MMC. Five of these were delivered to Abellio in March 2019 and put to use on the 207 (Hayes Bypass–White City) from Hayes, although the allocation moved to nearby Great Western Road, Southall in July 2019. Registered YX19ORG/H/J/K/L, these were numbered in 2001 to 2005, Abellio starting a new numbering series for these smart hybrids. Later in the year an order was placed for an additional forty-eight E40D smart hybrids for routes 482, 270, 285 and a part-conversion of route 278.

Those used for route 278 (Heathrow Central–Ruislip Station) were first to arrive, doing so in December 2019. These followed on from those allocated to the 207, becoming 2006 to 2012. They were allocated to Hayes garage carrying registration marks SN69ZRL/O/P/R/T/U/V. They worked the 278 alongside older Enviro 400s.

Route U5 once again changed garages in 2019. From 30 March 2523-31 transferred with the route from Hayes to Fulwell. Enviro 400 MMCs 2515-22 and 2532/3 transferred in April from Walworth to Hayes for use on the 207 and N207.

A new garage was opened at Armstrong Way, Great Western Park, Southall on 13 July 2019. This caused a number of movements in West London. First was the move of the 207/N207 from 23 July, transferring from Hayes to this new garage and the transfer of Enviro 400 MMCs 2515-22/32/3 to this new facility. 2523 to 2531 moved from Fulwell to Hayes with routes 350 and U5. 2501 to 2505 were also moved from Hayes to Southall on this date, also for use on the 207 and N207. The final movements for 2019 happened in August. 2580 to 2587 made the move from Walworth to Beddington. They were used, alongside 'classic' Enviro 400s 2401-3/5-10, to convert route 407 (Sutton-Caterham) to hybrid buses.

Three batches of E40D smart hybrid double-deckers arrived in 2020. The first nine arrived in March for use on the 482 (Southall Town Centre–Heathrow Airport Terminal 5). They were numbered 2013 to 2021 by Abellio and were registered YX20OBU/V/W/Y/Z, OCA-D. They were allocated to Hayes garage.

2022 to 2036 (SK20AZL/N/O/P/R/T/U/V/W/X/Z, BAA/O/U/V) were delivered to the company over the summer months. Abellio took over the 270 (Putney Bridge Station–Mitcham Commonside West) from Go-Ahead London from 30 May 2020, with 2022-36 being allocated to Beddington for use on the route. 2022-30 arrived in May, followed by 2033-6 in August and 2031/2 in September.

The final smart Hybrid Enviro 400 MMCs also arrived over the summer. These followed on as 2037 to 2053 and were registered (SK20BDZ, BEJ/O/U/Y, BFA/E/F/J/L/M/N/O/P/U/V/X). 2037-40/2/5/6 were taken into stock in July, with 2041/3/4/8/9 following in August. Delivery was complete in September when 2047/50-3 were delivered to Abellio. Fulwell was the recipient of these buses. They were put to use on the 285 (Kingston–Heathrow Central). 2013-53 were the first buses in the Abellio London fleet to use camera technology in place of traditional mirrors.

Hayes garage closed 11 December 2021. This led to the transfer of Enviro 400 MMCs 2006 to 2021 from Hayes to near-by Southall.

Abellio were successful in winning the contract for the 63 (King's Cross–Honor Oak) and N63 from Go-Ahead London, taking it on from 13 November 2021. For the route, twenty-nine Enviro 400 EV City bodied BYD D8UR DD buses were ordered. These were numbered 3401 to 3429 and were allotted registration marks LC71KWJ-P/R-Z, KXA/B/D-H/J-O. 3401/2/4/5/7-9 were first to arrive in November, followed by 3403/6/10-24 in December. 3425-9 were the last members to arrive, doing so in February 2022. All twenty-nine were allocated to Walworth. Traditional Enviro 400 MMCs filled in on the route until all had been taken into stock.

**Clapham Junction** finds 2548 (YY16YKP), one of eighteen Enviro 400 MMCs taken into stock during August 2016 for route 344.

**Route 427 was** the next Abellio service to receive the Enviro 400 MMC. Twenty-five were taken into stock for use on the route including 2562 (YX17NVJ), which is seen passing Ealing Hospital on its way to Uxbridge.

**A route** swap took place in 2017 between the 350 and U5. The fleet of Enviro 400 MMCs on the 350 moved onto the U5, this requiring additional vehicles. 2579 (YX17NPV) is the last of three additional MMCs taken into stock by Abellio London to cater for the need for extra vehicles. It is seen at Hayes & Harlington on its way to Uxbridge. 2579 was also one of a handful of buses on the route to have branding applied as seen on the upper deck window.

**Forty-one Enviro** 400 MMCs were taken into stock in 2017 and 2018 to operate routes 45 and 196. 2599 (YY67GZV) was one allocated to the 45. 2609 (SN18KKY) is seen operating the 196. Both are photographed passing through Elephant and Castle. The two batches were used indiscriminately on both services.

**Five Enviro** 400 MMC Smart Hybrid double-deckers were put to use by Abellio London on the 207. 2004 (YX19ORK) is photographed at Shepherds Bush Green, going to start up service on the route.

**Forty-eight Smart** Hybrid Enviro 400 MMCs were ordered to convert three routes to the type, as well as partially converting route 278 to the type. 2012 (SN69ZRV) was one of seven taken into stock at Hayes for the part-conversion of the route. It is photographed on its way to Heathrow Central whilst passing through Hayes & Harlington.

**Route 482 was** next to be converted to the Enviro 400 MMC Smart Hybrids. 2020 (YX20OCC) was the penultimate member of the batch allocated and is seen at Hatton Cross bus station on its way to Heathrow Terminal 5.

**Enviro 400 MMC** Smart Hybrid 2028 (SK20AZU) is photographed at journeys end at Putney Bridge.

**The final** route to be converted to the Enviro 400 MMC Smart Hybrid was the 285 between Kingston and Heathrow Central. 2038 (SK20BEJ) is captured by the camera about to pass Cromwell Road Bus Station, Kingston. The COVID-19 Pandemic of 2020/2021 led to a restriction on the number of passengers that buses were able to carry. This is shown by the stickers applied to the doors.

Enviro 400 MMC 2567 suffered an engine fire on 1 February, which caused severe damage to the bus. It was sold for scrap in June 2022.

Enviro 400 MMCs 2537-9/42-51 transferred in April from Walworth to Battersea. This allowed the type to convert route 415 (Tulse Hill Station–Old Kent Road) from the New Bus for London back to the Enviro 400 MMC, in turn releasing a number of New Bus for London's from the 415 to convert the 111 in West London to the latter type.

Several Enviro 400 MMCs received all-over advertising liveries during the summer. 2006 and 2007 gained advertisements for the Elizabeth Line in May, retaining these until March 2023. An advertisement for Verkada was applied to 2538 in June, being carried by this bus until October. 2022. June saw Her Majesty Queen Elizabeth II celebrated her Platinum Jubilee. To celebrate, a number of London buses were decorated in a smart purple and white livery. One of these buses was Enviro 400 MMC 2022, being decorated in May and keeping the livery until September.

2523-31 transferred from Hayes to a newly built garage at Dawley Road, Hayes in May.

Another twelve Enviro 400 EV City bodied BYD D8UR DD buses were taken into stock by Abellio in May 2022. 3430-41 (LG22APK/O/U/V/X/Y/Z, ARF/O/U/X/Z) were allocated to Dawley Road for use on the U5.

The introduction of these BYDs on the U5 led to the cascade of 2523-8/30 from Dawley Road to Battersea in June. Their arrival at the latter garage allowed Dennis Tridents to be replaced on the 345 (Peckham–South Kensington).

3401 (LC71KWJ) received the annual Poppy Appeal livery in October 2022, retaining it until November. 3424 (LC71KXJ) received a green-based all-over advertisement for OVO Energy in December. It lost this livery in the following August.

A handful of Enviro 400 MMCs left Southall garage in the early part of 2023, being transferred within Abellio for further use. 2572 and 2574 moved to Beddington in February, whilst 2569/70/1/3/6 moved to Battersea in March. 2575 also made the move to Battersea in May, with 2530 moving back to Hayes the same month.

2543 received an all-over advertisement for Puma / Noah in June 2023. It lost this livery the following month.

The closing months of 2022 saw a number of Wrightbus Streetdeck Electroliner double-deckers enter the Abellio fleet. Although they had been taken into stock to convert the 111 to the type, twelve of them were temporarily allocated to Dawley Road, Hayes for use on the U5. This in turn allowed several BYD D8UR DDs to transfer to Walworth for use on the 68. This took place in February when 3432-7 made the move. They returned to Dawley Road in June.

3401 to 3403 had a blue and green livery applied in February, promoting route 63. This livery was worn by the trio until April. A month later, in March, 3438 was briefly repainted into Super Loop livery to promote the new scheme. Super Loop was a new set of express services linking a number of locations in the suburbs of Greater London, the routes linking at various major hubs.

3406 was decorated into an all-over advertisement for London for Everyone in June. At the same time 3422 was a second Abellio bus to be given an advertisement for OVO Energy. 3422 retained this advertisement until June 2024 when it was put back into red livery. 3416 was used to promote its Zero Emissions credentials in July. Standard MMC 2034 (SK20BAO) was adorned with an advertisement for the £1.75 Hopper Fare in October. This livery was retained until March 2024.

Abellio London relaunched itself as Transport UK in December. Buses in the Abellio London fleet began to receive new company logos.

Four Enviro 400 MMCs were used to promote Suntory 196 Soda in May 2024. These buses were numbered 2607, 2614, 2615 and 2617. They retained this livery until June (2614/7), July (2607) or August (2615) when they were repainted red. 2542 was used by Transport UK to promote San Miguel in September, while 3406 lost its London for Everyone all-over livery.

**November 2021** saw Abellio London take on route 63 from Go-Ahead London. Abellio purchased twenty-nine electric BYD D8UR DDs which carried the Enviro 400EV City body style. 3423 (LC71KXH) is seen on its way to King's Cross in Peckham town centre carrying 'I am an electric bus' branding.

**The U5** was converted to the BYD D8UR DD in May 2022. 3437 (LG22ARF) is photographed entering Uxbridge Station on its way to Hayes & Harlington Station.

**The first** three (3401-3) Enviro 400EV City bodied BYD D8UR DDs were adorned with route branding for route 63. The last of the three, 3403 (LC71KWL) is photographed outside St Pancras International at the start of its journey to Honor Oak.

**3406 (LC71KWO)** was decorated in an all-over advertisement for London for Everyone in June 2022. It is seen carrying this smart livery as it joins Euston Road on its way to Honor Oak. Both the British Library and the Pancras Hotel can be seen in the background.

**The relaunch** of Abellio London in December 2023 to Transport UK brought with it a new logo. This is seen applied to 2011 (SN69ZRU), which is seen crossing the bridge over the rail lines at Hayes & Harlington.

**The Transport** UK can also be seen applied to BYD/ Enviro 400EV City 3414 (LC71KWX). It is seen starting its journey at St Pancras, heading south towards Honor Oak.

**3422 (LC71KXG)** was one of a number of London buses that were used to advertise OVO Energy. It is also seen heading towards Honor Oak at St Pancras.

# METROLINE

Metroline purchased a large number of the classic Enviro 400 model to replace its sizable fleet of Plaxton President buses. Alongside the Enviro 400s, a large quantity of Wrightbus Gemini 2 and Gemini 3 buses were also purchased, these being based on Volvo chassis.

A small number of Enviro 400 MMCs were taken into stock in early 2015. These were numbered TEH2072 to TEH2087 by the company. These were registered LK15CWA/C, CRZ, CSF/O/U/V/X/Y/Z, CTE/F, CUA/C/G/H. February saw the arrival of TEH2072/3, with the rest being delivered in March. They were taken into stock for route 332 (Paddington–Neasden Tesco) from Cricklewood. They were also frequently found operating the 189. Other than a refurbishment, very little of interest happened with these buses.

Metroline received two batches of Enviro 400EV City bodied BYD D8UR DDs. The first was made up of thirty-seven of the type and were delivered over the course of 2019 and were put to use on the 43 (London Bridge–Friern Barnet). The first five arrived in May registered LJ19CTY/Z, CUA/C/G/H/K/W. They were allotted rolling stock numbers BDE2614 to BDE2619, BDE2620/4. BDE2623/6/7/8/32/3/4/6/9 (LJ19CUW/Y, CVA/B/F/G/H/L/O) were next to arrive in July. BDE2631/5/43/5 (LJ19CVE/K/T/V) followed in August.

BDE2641/2/4/6/7 (LJ19CVR/S/U/W/X) arrived in September, with BDE2638 LJ19CVN, 2640 LJ19CVP, 2648 LJ19CVY, 2649 LJ19CVZ all arriving in October. The order for thirty-seven was completed in November when BDE2613 (LJ19CTX) was delivered to Metroline. These measured 10.9m in length. All were stored at Willesden Junction before entering service from Holloway. Of these vehicles, BDE2613-9/35/8/40-9 were fitted with windows on the stairwell, whilst BDE2620-34/6/7/9 were not.

Demonstrator LF69UXJ was placed on loan to Metroline in July 2020. It covered for the above fleet of BDEs whilst they underwent warranty work.

BDE2627 was the first BYD in London to receive an all-over advertisement. In October 2021 it was used to promote FFI green energy. It retained this advertisement until February 2022. BDE2632 (LJ19CUV) was the second in the Metroline fleet to receive an all-over advertisement. It was used to promote OVO Energy in March 2022, keeping this livery until April 2023. It was at this time it received a second advertisement, this time for the 'Who Gives a Crap' toilet tissue brand. BDE2637 received an all-over advertisement in May 2022 for Evian, keeping this until July. along with two further advertisements received by the BDEs. At this time BDE2620 promoted San Pellegrino and BDE2629 for Bananas. These were lost in October 2022 and February 2023 respectively.

Seventeen BYDs arrived over the summer of 2022. These were numbered BDE2752 to BDE2768 which carried registration marks LG22AXF/H/J/K/M/N/O/P/R/S/T/U/

V/W/X/Y/Z. BDE2752-6 arrived in July, the others being taken into stock in August. Destined for Edgware, they were stored at West Perivale waiting for the electric supply to be installed at their intended garage. They started to enter service in March 2023 on route 142 (Brent Cross–Watford Junction).

Three all-over advertisements were applied to the BYD fleet in 2023. BDE2618 was decorated in an advertisement for BDE2618 in January 2023, retaining this livery until August. BDE2637 was second to receive a livery in May, this time for Evian. BDE2621 was a second of the type to receive an advertisement for OVO Energy in July, this being replaced by a revised version in February 2024. BDE2621 lost this livery in July 2024. BDE2646 was used to promote its Zero Emissions credentials in August 2023. It retained this livery until February 2024 when it was repainted red. An all-over advertisement for McCains was applied to BDE2640 in March, retaining this livery until May, with BDE2626 gaining an all-over advertisement promoting its Zero Emissions credentials in August.

In September 2024, Metroline placed an order for forty-six Enviro 400 EV City bodied BYDs for operation on routes 206 (Willesden Junction), 210 (Cricklewood) and W8 (Potters Bar). Fleet numbers BDE2985 to BDE3030 were allocated to these buses.

**Sixteen Enviro** 400 MMCs were taken into stock in 2015 for use on the 332. TEH2077 (LK15CSU) is seen in Kilburn on its way to Paddington.

**The Enviro** 400 MMCs used on the 332 often found themselves operating journeys on the 139. TEH2080 (LK15CSY) is found at Tennyson Way, Waterloo whilst heading to West Hampstead on the 139.

**Holloway Road** finds BDE2616 (LJ19CUA) on its way to Friern Barnet. This was one that kept the windows on the stairwell.

**London Bridge** is the southern terminus of route 43. It is this location that we find BDE2627 (LJ19CVA), seen setting off for its journey north to Friern Barnet.

**A number** of the BYDs had the windows on the stairwells covered by advertisements. This is shown by BDE2630 (LJ19CVD) which is also captured by the camera at Holloway Road.

**The next** batch of BDE-class Enviro 400EV City double-deckers arrived in 2022, although they did not enter service until the spring of 2023, being used on the 142. BDE2752 (LG22AXF) is photographed entering Edgware bus station on its way to Brent Cross Shopping Centre.

**BDE2757 (LG22AXN)** also represents the fleet of BDE-class Enviro 400EV City double-deckers that were used on the 142 by Metroline. Edgware again provides the backdrop for this photograph. BDE2757 is seen operating a short working the 142, terminating at West Hendon Broadway.

# STAGECOACH LONDON

The first Enviro 400 MMC double decks to enter the Stagecoach London fleet arrived between May and July 2015. Twenty-one Enviro 400 MMCs arrived with Selkent during this period based on the Volvo B5LH hybrid chassis. Rolling stock numbers 13061 to 13081 were allocated to these buses which carried registration marks BF15KGK/N/P/U/V/X/Y/Z, KHB/C/D/G/H/J, BJ15TVZ, TWA, BF15KHA, BJ15TWC, BF15KGJ/O, KHE. 13061 and 13062 were first to arrive in May, with 13063-75/7-9 following in June. 13076/80/1 were last to arrive, putting in an appearance in July. Initially stored at West Ham these twenty-one MMCs were allocated to Plumstead for use on the 177 (Peckham–Thamesmead).

A month later, the first integral Enviro 400 MMCs were delivered to Stagecoach East London. Seven were allocated to North Street, Romford for use on the 498 (Brentwood Sainsburys – Romford Queen's Hospital). These were conventional E40D diesel models and were allocated fleet numbers 10301 to 10307 and registered YY15OYS-X/Z. 10301 and 10302 arrived in June, with the outstanding vehicles being delivered in July.

The end of 2015, beginning of 2016, saw the arrival of a second consignment of Enviro 400 MMCs based on the Volvo B5LH chassis, these also being the last of this combination to be purchased for Stagecoach London, these again joining the Selkent division. 13082 to 13102 were allocated to Catford for use on the 47 (Shoreditch–Bellingham, Catford Bus Garage). Registered BL65OYA-H/J/K/M-P/R/T-Y, 13082-91 were delivered to the company in December 2015, with 13092-102 arriving in January 2016.

Stagecoach East London received forty diesel Enviro 400 MMCs during the spring of 2016, these being split between Barking and North Street, Romford. 10308 to 10332 (SN16OJM/O/P/R/S-Z, OKA-D/F-H/J-M/O/P) were those allocated to Barking, these being used to convert route 62 (Barking–Marks Gate) from single-deck to double-deck operation, as well as forming part of the allocation on route 145 (Leytonstone Station–Dagenham Asda). 10333 to 10347 (SN16OKR/S/T/U/V/W/X/Z, OLB/C/G/H/J/K/O) were allocated to North Street, Romford for use on the 294 (Havering Park–Noak Hill). 10308/10-3/5/26-32 were delivered to the company in March, with 10309/14/6-25/33-47 following in April.

**13066 (BF15KGX)** is one of twenty-one Enviro 400 MMC bodied Volvo B5LHs to enter service with Stagecoach London on the 177. It is seen passing through Woolwich town centre whilst heading towards Thamesmead.

**The fleet** of Volvo B5LHs could also be found operating on other services from Plumstead garage. 13061 (BF15KGK) is captured by the camera in Lewisham town centre on its way to Crystal Palace whilst operating route 122.

**The first** Enviro 400 MMC bodied E40Ds entered service from North Street, Romford on the 498. The last of these, 10307 (YY15OYZ), is seen in Romford town centre.

**A second** batch of Enviro 400 MMC bodied Volvo B5LHs were taken into stock by Stagecoach London at the end of 2015, beginning of 2016. Allocated to Catford they were predominantly used on the 47. 13097 (BL65OYT) represents these double-deckers. It seen heading towards Catford bus garage, known as Bellingham, passing through Lewisham town centre.

**13088 (BL65OYG)** is seen off route, operating the 136. It is photographed nearing the end of its journey at Elephant & Castle.

**Barking took** stock of twenty-five Enviro 400 MMCs in March and April 2016. 10309 (SN16OJO) is seen operating the 62 passing through Barking town centre.

**The twenty-five** Enviro 400 MMCs were also used to partially convert the 145 to the type. 10325 (SN16OKG) is photographed in Ilford whilst heading towards Leytonstone.

**Another fifteen** Enviro 400 MMCs were allocated to North Street, Romford for route 294. 10336 (SN16OKU) is seen passing Romford Station on its way to Noak Hill.

The first integral hybrid Enviro 400 MMC E40H double-decks entered the fleet in the summer of 2016. Totalling thirty-six they were allocated to Stagecoach Selkent at Plumstead. Numbered 12365-400 they carried registration marks YX16OGD-H/J-P/R-W/Y/Z, OHA-H/J-L/N-P/R/S. 12365/7/70-80/2/5/7/8/91 arrived in June, with 12366/8/9/81/3/4/6/9/90/2-400 following in July. Initially stored at West Ham, these were used on route 53 (Plumstead–Whitehall, Horse Guards), displacing older diesel buses which transferred to North Street, Romford.

Three additional E40D models arrived with Stagecoach Selkent during September 2016. Following on from similar vehicles delivered to North Street, Romford in April, the trio took up fleet numbers 10348-50 and carried registration marks YX66WCU/T/R. They were allocated to Catford where they were used to cover an increase in the pvr (peak vehicle requirement) on the 199 (Canada Water–Bellingham,, Catford Bus Garage). They could also be found operating alongside similar bodied Volvo B5LH buses on the 47.

A solitary MMC bodied E40H hybrid double-decker, numbered 12401 (YX66WCP), arrived in June. As with the above two double-decks, 12401 was ordered by the company to help with an increase on the 75 (Lewisham–Croydon). Joining 10348-50 at Catford, it could also be found operating on other double-deck routes from Catford as required. A second similar Enviro 400 MMC arrived in October, again for Selkent. 12402 (YX66WAU) was allocated to Plumstead where it was used to cover an increase in the pvr on route 177.

The opening months of 2017 saw the arrival of twenty-three Enviro 400 MMC bodied E40H hybrids. 12403-25 (YY66PHA/F/J/K/N/O/U/V/X/Z, PJJ/O/U/V/X, PKA/C-F, YY66PXT-V) were allocated to Stagecoach East London's Bow garage to upgrade the rolling stock on the 277 (Highbury & Islington–Crossharbour Asda). 12403-9 arrived in January with 12410-25 following in February. 12417 (YY66PJX) was allocated registration mark, 527CLT, in April 2017, this previously being carried by Scania N230UD OmniCity 15100.

Four Enviro 400 MMCs in the Stagecoach London fleet were repainted into a lime green based all-over advertisement for World Environment Day, these being 10301, 10324, 13070 and 13087 respectively. 10324 returned to standard red livery in July, with the other three following in August.

The final new MMCs to arrive in 2017 did so in September. Seven E40H models were taken into stock by Stagecoach East London's Leyton garage. Numbered 12426 to 12432 they were registered YX67VBC-G/J/K and were used to top up the fleet used on the 257 (Stratford Bus Station–Walthamstow Central Station).

Stagecoach Selkent took on the contract for the 161 (North Greenwich–Chislehurst) from Go-Ahead London's Metrobus division on 17 March 2018. To operate the route, nineteen Enviro 400 MMC bodied E40Hs were ordered, these arriving with the company in February 2018. 12433 to 12451 (SN67XDW-Z, XEB-H/J-M/O/P/R/S) were operated by the company from Plumstead.

Since 2016, Transport for London (TfL) have advertised its investment in hybrid buses by decorating certain vehicles in a so-called 'green bus' livery, advertising the number of 'green' vehicles operating in London. This livery was applied to 13090 (BL65OYJ) in April 2018, the bus retaining this livery until June. A second MMC, 10301, was adorned with an all-over advertisement in June 2018. It was repainted green to promote the Macmillan Cancer Trust. It was named *Martyn Henderson*, after a Romford driver who had died from cancer in 2017. In August, 10301 was re-registered from YY15OYS to WLT546. 10301 received an updated version of the livery in November 2022.

Delivery of Enviro 400 MMCs switched from the E40H model to the newly introduced E40D Smart Hybrid model from the summer of 2018. Fifty-four of the type were first of the type to enter service from Stagecoach East London's West Ham garage on routes 330 (Wanstead Park–Canning Town) and 474 (Canning Town–Manor Park). They were delivered out of sequence, with 11033-54 (SN18KTX, KUA-H/J/K, YY18TGF/J/K/N/O/U/V/X/Z, THF/G) arriving in June. 11001-9 arrived in July, whilst 11010-20 were delivered to the company in August. Delivery was complete in September when 11021-32 arrived with the company. 11001-32 were registered YY18TKZ, TLF/J/K/N/U/V/X/Z, TMO/U/V/X/Z, TNE/F, YX68UKA/B/D-H/J-P/R/S. 11033 to 11040 were loaned to Stagecoach Midlands in July prior to entering service in London, these being used on the annual Silverstone British Grand Prix shuttle services. Before entering service, 11001-16 were re-allocated to Catford for use on the 136 (Grove Park Station–Elephant & Castle), this being a result of the introduction of a low-emission bus zone in the Lewisham and Catford areas of south-east London by the Mayor of London.

The type gained a large presence in the Stagecoach London fleet, with another 121 E40D Smart Hybrids entering the fleet between September 2018 and August 2020.

The first nine arrived in September 2018 to complete the allocation of the type on the 136 from Catford, these working alongside 11001-16. These were numbered 11055 to 11063 (YX68UMU-W/Y/Z, UNB/E/F/G).

Eleven more arrived with Stagecoach Selkent in December, being added to Bromley's allocation. These followed on from the September arrivals, becoming 11064 to 11074 (YX68UTG/H/J-P/R/T). These were put to use on the 261 between Lewisham and Princess Royal Hospital.

The next thirty-five were taken into stock, again by Stagecoach Selkent, between January and March 2019. Numbered 11301 to 11335 they were allocated to Catford for use on routes 54 (Woolwich–Elmers End Station) and 75.

These were registered in three different registration series, with registration marks SO68HDJ-L/N/U/V/X/Y, SK19EKX/Y/Z, ELC/H/J/O/U, YW68PCV/U/O/F, PBZ, OWL-P/R-V/X, PAO, PBF/O being carried.

Seven found themselves allocated to Stagecoach East London's Rainham garage in May 2019 for use on the 372 (Hornchurch–Lakeside Shopping Centre). Numbered 11075 to 11081 (YX19OMA/C-H) they did not enter service on the 372 until June, being used on Docklands Light Railway replacement work prior to this.

The final, and largest batch, arrived with Stagecoach London between April and August 2020. Fifty-nine arrived between this period to convert routes 25 (Holborn Circus–Ilford Broadway), N25 and 425 (Clapton, Nightingale Road–Ilford, Hainault Street). These Enviro 400 MMCs were allocated to Bow, and to make way for their arrival 12403 to 12425 were re-allocated along with route 277 from Bow to West Ham in June. 11341 to 11375 (SK20AXT-Z, AYA-D/F-H/J/L-P/S-Z) arrived in April and May for use on the 25 and N25. 11376 to 11399 (SK20BBE/F/J/N/O/U/V/X/Z, BCE/F/O/U/V/X-Z, BDE/F/O/U/V/X/Y) were delivered in July (11376-83) and August (11384-99). These were the official fleet of vehicles for use on the 425. Although each of the routes had specific vehicles allocated to them, the fifty-nine Enviro 400 MMCs were intermixed on both routes.

The takeover of the 425 took place on 4 July 2020, and as mentioned above some of the intended fleet of Enviro 400 MMCs were not delivered until August. This meant that there were not enough buses available to operate the route. To compensate, 11035-8 were loaned to Bow from West Ham, and 11069/70/2/3 from Bromley.

However, this was done during the COVID-19 Pandemic of 2020, meaning that the weekday operation of these routes were running to a Sunday timetable.

The first of forty-seven AD Enviro 400EV City bodied BYD D8UR DD buses entered the Stagecoach East London fleet in November 2020. These vehicles were allocated to Rainham for use on routes 173 (King George's Hospital–Beckton DLR Station), 174 (Harold Hill–Dagenham, Marsh Way) and school route 673. Rolling stock numbers 14101 to 14147 were allocated to these double-deckers along with registration marks LF70YTV/W-Z, YUA-E/G/H/J-L/N/O/R/S/U/V-Y, YVA-E/G/H/J-P/R-Z. 14001-6 and 14130-9 arrived in November 2020 and were initially placed in storage at West Ham. 14107/0 followed in December. 14110/1/3-6/8/9/25/8 arrived in February 2021, with 14112/7/20-4/6/7/9 completing delivery in March.

A further twenty-seven Enviro 400EV City' arrived in November and December 2021. These followed on from the Rainham vehicles, becoming 14148 to 14172 (LG71DNV/X/Y, DOA/H/J/U, DPE/F/K/N/O/U/V/X-Z, DRO/V/X/Z, DSE/O/U/V). These were split between Catford (14148-62) and Plumstead (14163-72). Those allocated to Catford were used on routes 160 (Catford Bridge Station–Sidcup Station) and 660, with the Plumstead allocation entering service on the 180 (Lewisham–Belvedere Industrial Area).

Enviro 400 MMCs 11005 and 11363 were used to promote the 2021 Poppy Appeal livery in October 2021, losing it, naturally, towards the end of November when the appeal was over for another year.

Six of the BYDs and two of the Smart Hybrid Enviro 400 MMCs were treated to all-over advertisements between November 2021 and December 2022. 14147 was the first, being adorned with one for FFI in November, retaining this livery until January 2022. An advertisement for Evian was applied to 14129 in May, with 14129 retaining this livery until June. 14170 was a second BYD to gain an advertisement during May. It was used to promote the newly opened Elizabeth Line, retaining this until December 2022. Smart Hybrids 11031 and 11053 both received similar all-over advertisements for the Elizabeth Line at the same time, also retaining the livery until December 2022. 14141 was used to promote San Pellegrino between August and December 2022. 14105 was Stagecoach's choice to promote the 2022 Poppy Appeal, wearing an advertisement between October and November 2022. 14160 was the final BYD to be adorned with an all-over advertisement in 2022, doing so in December. It was used to promote OVO Energy until December 2023.

The Stagecoach Group acquired two operators in the London area in the summer of 2022. One of these was Hackney Community Transport (CT Plus). From 27 August 2022 158 buses transferred to Stagecoach London. These included forty-nine AD Enviro 400 City bodied E40Hs and a pair of Enviro 400EV City bodied BYD D8UR DDs. Numbered 2501 to 2549 and 2550e and 2551e with their former operator, these became 12501-49 and 14173 and 14174 in the Stagecoach London fleet. Registration marks for these buses can be found under the Hackney Community Transport chapter later in this book or in Appendix I.

BYDs 14111 and 14127 were the first of their type to receive an alternative livery in 2023. They both received an advertisement for OVO Energy in January.

To make way for the large number of electric buses ordered for the Stagecoach group, Stagecoach renumbered their existing electric buses. 14101 to 14174 were renumbered to 84101-74 in April 2023.

Just after the renumbering took place, 84148 (former 14148) had a dark blue livery applied and was used to celebrate the coronation of King Charles III, keeping this livery until July. A month later 84113 (14113) was adorned with an advertisement for Evian.

11342 was the next MMC to adorn an all-over advertisement. In September it was used to promote Fenty Beauty. The following month, 11362 was used to promote the £1.75 hopper fare being offered by TfL. The same month saw former CT Plus Enviro 400 City 12538 adorned with an all-over advertisement for the annual Poppy Appeal, losing this livery in November. 84127 and 84160 lost their all-over advertisements for OVO energy in October and December 2023 respectively.

In February 2024 there was a swap around of some of Stagecoach London's Enviro 400 MMC fleet. From 24 February, the company won the contract for the 242/N242 (Homerton Hospital–Aldgate Bus Station) from Arriva London. 11017-20/2-5/7-9/31-3 transferred from West Ham to Ash Grove for the take up of the route prior to new rolling stock arriving for the 242. These buses were replaced on the 277 by 12408 to 12425 from routes 330 and 474.

Barking based 12400 (YX16OHS) was repainted in a white, red, black and silver livery in March 2024, this being a pre-1933 livery. It became the East London Ambassador.

In May, a pair of Enviro 400 MMCs were used to promote Northeastern Uni. The vehicles concerned were numbered 11352 and 11376, which kept this livery until July (11352) and August (11376) respectively. In August, 11373 was used to promote tourism to Thailand. During the same month, 11399 gained an advertisement to promote that it is a low emissions bus. 11066 received a special livery in September, becoming the Selkent Ambassador, wearing a special red, white and black livery similar to 12400 mentioned above. 11360 was used to promote San Miguel in September; with similar 11383 being used to promote White Fox during the same month.

**The first** Enviro 400 MMC bodied E40H integral hybrid buses to enter service with Stagecoach were allocated to Plumstead for use on the 53. 12366 (YX16OGE) is photographed at Parliament Square about to enter Whitehalll.

**Route 53 is** one of a number of routes that use Elephant & Castle to access south London. 12376 (YX16OGP) is seen at this location on its way to Plumstead Station.

**In September** 2016, three additional Enviro 400 MMC bodied E40Ds were taken into stock to cover an increase in requirement on the 199. 10350 (YX66WCR) is seen in Lewisham heading to Canada Water.

**12401 (YX66WCP)** was one of a pair of Enviro 400 MMC bodied E40Hs taken into stock by Stagecoach London to cover an increase in vehicle requirements. It is photographed in Woolwich on route 54 shortly before terminating.

**12402 (YX66WAU)** was the second member of the pair taken into stock to cover an increase in demand. Allocated to Plumstead it is seen at Elephant & Castle on its way to Plumstead Station.

**Route 277 gained** a fleet of Enviro 400 MMCs in the first part of 2017. 12407 (YY66PHN) was one of these buses and is seen travelling through Mile End towards Crossharbour.

**Another of** the 277 batch, 12417, is seen on Bishopsgate off route on the 205. It is seen carrying cherished registration mark 527CLT which it received in April 2017.

**10324 (SN16OKF)** was one of four Enviro 400 MMCs that were used to promote World Environment Day in June 2017, for which a lime-green based livery was chosen. It is seen in Ilford town centre heading towards Leytonstone on route 145.

**13087 (BL65OYF)** was another of the four buses chosen to promote World Environment Day. It is seen passing under the railway lines at Lewisham Station heading towards Bellingham, Catford Bus Garage.

**Seven E40Hs** were taken into stock during September 2017 seeing service on the 257. 12429 (YX67VBF) is photographed entering Stratford bus station.

**Route 161 was** won from Metrobus in 2017. For the route a fleet of nineteen Enviro 400 MMC bodied E40Hs were taken into stock by Stagecoach London. 12435 (SN67XDY) is photographed at Woolwich heading towards North Greenwich.

**Woolwich also** finds 12446 (SN67XEL), heading in the opposite direction to Chislehurst.

**In June** 2018, 10301 (YY15OYS) had a green based livery applied to promote MacMillan Cancer Support. August 2018 saw the bus gain new registration mark WLT546. It is photographed passing under the rail bridges in Romford, about to pass Romford Station.

**11001-16 were** originally to have been allocated to West Ham garage. However, the introduction of a low-emission bus zone in Lewisham meant that these buses were reallocated to Catford garage for the 136. The first of these, 11001 (YY18TKZ), is photographed in Lewisham town centre on its way to Elephant & Castle.

**11017-54 were** allocated to West Ham for a number of routes centred on the Canning Town area. 11024 (YX68UKJ) is seen entering Canning Town bus station on its way to Stratford City.

**Route 330 was** one of the routes to benefit from the fleet of Smart Hybrid Enviro 400 MMCs. 11041 (SN18KUH) is photographed on layover at Canning Town Bus Station.

**474 was** another route to be converted to the Smart Hybrid Enviro 400 MMC. The Canning Town DLR and London Underground station provides the backdrop to 11049 (YY18TGU) which is seen heading towards Manor Park.

**Nine additional** E40D Smart Hybrids arrived for use on the 136 at Catford. 11059 (YX68UMZ) was one of these buses, and is seen operating route 75, photographed in Lewisham town centre.

**In December** 2018 eleven smart hybrids were taken into stock at Bromley for use on the 261. 11067 (YX68UTK) is seen on its way to Lewisham, passing through the northern part of Bromley town centre.

**Route 54 and** 75 were won from Metrobus in early 2019. Thirty-five Enviro 400 MMCs were allocated to Catford for use on the two routes. 11313 (SK19ELH) is seen crossing the tram tracks before reaching the terminus of route 75 at Croydon town centre.

**11316 (SK19ELU)** is photographed passing through Lewisham on its way to Elmers End on route 54.

**Route 372 was** upgraded to the Enviro 400 MMC in June 2019. 11077 (YX19OMD) represents the fleet of seven that were allocated to Rainham for the route. It is photographed in Hornchurch town centre on its way to Lakeside.

**11353 (SK20AYG)** was one of fifty-nine Enviro 400 MMCs taken into stock at Bow during 2020 for use on the 25 and 425. It is captured by the camera departing Stratford bus station on its way to Ilford.

**Aldgate finds** another member of this large fleet of Enviro 400 MMCs, 11371 (SK20AZC). It is again seen heading northwards to Ilford.

**The fleet** of Enviro 400 MMCs used on the 25 and 425 could also be found on occasions operating the 8 and 205. 11380 (SK20BBO) is seen at Bishopsgate whilst operating a journey on the 8 towards Bow Church.

**11396 (SK20BDU)** is photographed at Stratford bus station whilst operating the 425 to Clapton, Nightingale Road. The 2020 Covid-19 pandemic caused restrictions to be placed on how many passengers buses could carry. This fleet of double-deckers were restricted to thirty passengers as denoted by the sticker on the entrance doors.

**In July** 2020, some buses were loaned to Bow to help out on the 425 due to the late arrival of some of the 11300s. 11036 (SN18KUC) was one of these buses, and is seen at Stratford on the 425 to Ilford.

**The first** electric double-deckers for Stagecoach London entered service on routes 173 and 174. These were in the form of the Enviro 400EV City bodied BYD DD8UR. The first of these, 14101 (LF70YTV), is seen at Dagenham Heathway on its way to Dagenham, Marsh Way.

**Advertisements for** OVO Energy were applied to a number of London Buses. 14111 (LF70YUG) represents the company as it passes Romford Station on its way to Dagenham, Marsh Way.

**Route 173 terminates** at the bus station opposite the Docklands Light Railway Station at Beckton. It is this location that we find 14123 (LF70YUX).

**A further** twenty-seven BYD electric double-deckers arrived in November and December 2021. Their arrival allowed a full conversion of route 160, operated from Catford, and a part-conversion of the 180 from Plumstead. 14153 (LG71DOJ) was one of those allocated to Catford for the 160. It seen on its way to Sidcup Station, passing Eltham Church.

**14169 (LG71DSE)** was one of ten BYDs allocated to Plumstead for route 180. It is seen heading to Belvedere when photographed in Woolwich town centre.

**Fifty-one Enviro** 400 City double-deckers were inherited by Stagecoach London from CT Plus on 27 August 2022. 12501 (SN16OHP) was the first numerically and is seen heading to London Bridge on the 388, one of three routes taken on. It is passing through a wet Bishopsgate.

**Route 26 was** the second route operated by Ash Grove. 12525 (SN66WRK) is again seen on Bishopsgate, heading northwards to Hackney Wick.

**Route 20 (Walthamstow–Debden)** was the third route inherited. This route was operated from the Walthamstow Stadium garage. 12545 (YX19ORW) is seen in Walthamstow, heading towards Debden.

**In April** 2023 Stagecoach renumbered their electric buses. 84164 (LG71DPZ), formerly 14164, is seen in Woolwich town centre on its way to Erith.

**For many** years Stagecoach have operated shuttle services to the British Grand Prix at the Silverstone circuit in Northamptonshire. Whilst the majority of buses used are from provincial fleets, Stagecoach London also provide some vehicles. 11013 (YY18TMX) and 10335 (SN16OKT) were amongst those used on the 2024 shuttles. They are photographed on layover outside Northampton Town Football Club's Sixfields Stadium in Northampton.

**12400 (YX16OHS)** was decorated in a red, white and black livery in August 2024 and named East London Ambassador. It is seen on its way to Leytonstone on route 145, passing its home garage of Barking. *Ben Everitt*

**11066 (YX68UTJ)** followed 12400 in gaining a special livery, being done in September. It was repainted in a similar livery as 12400 to celebrate the 100 years of Bromley bus garage. 11066 was named *Selkent Diplomat*. *Ben Everitt*

# GO-AHEAD LONDON

Go-Ahead London was made up of five operating companies; London Central, London General, Blue Triangle, Docklands Buses and Metrobus. All five operating companies received examples of the Enviro 400 MMC or the Enviro 400EV City.

Sixteen Enviro 400 MMCs were delivered in June 2016 for use on the 135 (Old Street–Crossharbour Asda), operating from the former Docklands Buses garage at Silvertown. EHV1-16 were initially stored at Northumberland Park before moving to their intended garage. Registration marks BK15AZR/T, BJ15TWL, BL15HBK, BJ15TWP, BL15HBJ/O/P/U/X/Y/Z, HCA/C/D and HBN were carried by these buses.

The next delivery of Enviro 400 MMCs arrived in March and April 2016. Twenty-two E40H models were allocated to Camberwell for use on the 35 (Clapham Junction–Shoreditch High Street), also seeing service on route 40 (Dulwich Library-Aldgate). These took up rolling stock numbers EH39 to EH60 (YX16OBT-W/Y/Z, OCA-H/J/L-P/S). EH39-46 arrived in March, with the others putting in an appearance in April. The batch started at EH39 as Go-Ahead London had already taken stock of thirty-eight of the classic Enviro 400 model on the E40H chassis.

Thirteen more arrived over the winter of 2016, these following on from the Camberwell vehicles. Numbered EH61 to EH73 (YX66WHC-H/J-N/P/R), these found service on the 363 (Crystal Palace–Elephant & Castle) from Peckham. EH61/2/5 arrived in October, the outstanding vehicles being delivered in November.

Putney High Street had become the most polluted street in London during the 2010s. To try and reduce the affect that buses had on this situation Go-Ahead London invested heavily in new buses for Putney garage. Among the new vehicles ordered for routes operating down Putney High Street were thirty-nine Enviro 400 MMCs based on the E40H chassis, although the original order called for them to be based on the Volvo B5LH chassis, with fleet numbers EHV17-55 being originally allocated. However, since they were based on the E40H chassis the new double-deckers took up rolling stock numbers EH74 to EH112. These buses were registered YY66OYB/C/E-H/J-P/R-X/Z, OZA-H/J-M/O/P/R-U and operated under the control of London General. EH74 was the only one to arrive in November. EH75-81/3/5/7, 92 followed in December. Delivery was complete in January 2017 when EH82/4/6/8-91/3-112 were taken into stock at Putney. These were ordered against operation on the 14 (Putney Heath–Warren Street Station), although could be found on any of the double-deck routes operating from Putney.

Eighteen E40Hs were taken into stock by London Central at Camberwell in January 2017. Numbered EH113 to EH130 (SN66WNY/Z, WOA-D/H/J/M/R/U/V/X/Y, WPA/D/E/F) they were ordered for use on the 42 (Liverpool Street–East Dulwich Sainsbury's) but were also used on other double-deck routes from Camberwell.

A pair of standard diesel E40D double-decks complete with Enviro 400 MMC bodywork were taken into stock in February. These were 10.9m in length and were built to single-door layout. Numbered E284 and E285 (SN66WNE/F) the pair wore the red with grey skirt livery and were allocated to the Commercial Services fleet and were initially allocated to London General's Sutton garage.

Go-Ahead London lays claim to applying the first all-over advertisement to an Enviro 400 MMC. The vehicle concerned was EH79, which received an all-over advertisement for the 2018 Winter Olympics in South Korea, this livery being applied in April 2017 and retained it until June. EH94 was the second of its type to gain an all-over advertisement, doing so in August 2017. It was used to promote Isabel Marant until October when it returned to red.

Two further batches of Enviro 400 MMC bodied E40Hs arrived during 2017. Thirty-one arrived in August at River Road, Barking to convert route 115 (Aldgate–East Ham) to the type and converting part of route 5 (Canning Town–Romford Market) to the type. EH131-61 (YW17JTV/X-Z, JUA/C/E/F/H/J/K/O/T/U/V/X/Y, JVA/C-H/J-P) were the vehicles taken into stock for this purpose.

The second consignment was made up of just nine EH-class Enviro 400 MMCs. These followed on as EH162 to EH170 (YX67VFG/H/J-P), these finding homes at Camberwell. These were taken into stock during October.

**The first** Enviro 400 MMCs to be taken into stock by Go-Ahead London were based on the Volvo B5LH chassis. EHV9 (BL15HBU) is seen on the 135 to Crossharbour at Liverpool Street.

**Twenty-four E40Hs** were taken into stock by Go-Ahead London and allocated to London Central's Camberwell garage. From there they were split between routes 35 and 40. EH41 (YX16OBV) is photographed crossing London Bridge on its way south to Clapham Common.

**EH54 (YX16OCL)** was another of the fleet allocated to the 35 and 40. It is photographed negotiating Elephant & Castle on its way to London Bridge.

**Thirteen more** followed for route 363, these being allocated to Peckham. EH67 (YX66WHJ) is photographed in Peckham town centre on its way to Crystal Palace.

**A large** number of Enviro 400 MMCs and Wright Gemini 2s were allocated to Putney during 2016. By this time Putney High Street had become one of the most polluted roads in London. EH88 (YY66OYS) represents part of this batch, seen about to cross Putney Bridge on its way to Putney Heath.

**Route 74 was** another of Putney's routes to be allocated a fleet of Enviro 400 MMCs in 2016. EH107 (YY66DZO) is seen rounding Marble Arch on its way to Baker Street.

**Route 42 Liverpool** Street–Denmark Hill) was the next route to be converted to the Enviro 400 MMC. EH126 (SN66WOY) was one of eighteen taken into stock at Camberwell for use on the route. It is photographed almost at journeys end at Liverpool Street.

**EH79 (YY66OYH)** was the first Enviro 400 MMC to be given an all-over advertisement. It was used to promote the 2018 Winter Olympics in South Korea. It is photographed on its way to Putney Heath on the 14 whilst rounding Hyde Park Corner.

**In August** 2017 EH94 (YY66OYZ) was adorned with an all-over advertisement for Isabel Marant. It is photographed carrying this advertisement whilst on the 430 to South Kensington whilst loading on Putney High Street.

**Two diesel** powered Enviro 400 MMCs for use in Go-Ahead London's commercial fleet arrived in February 2017. E285 (SN66WNF) is seen at St Pancras International whilst operating Wimbledon shuttles.

**EH132 (YW17JTX)** was one of a fleet of buses put to use on the 5 and 115 in East London. East Ham provides the backdrop to this photograph.

**Another member** of the 5/115 fleet is EH144 (YW17JUU). It is seen on route 5 to Romford Market whilst passing Barking railway station.

**Romford Station** finds EH146 (YW17JUX). The 5 and 115 were operated by the Blue Triangle subsidiary, as can be seen by the fleet name worn by EH146.

2018 saw no less than 140 Enviro 400 MMC bodied E40Hs ordered by Go-Ahead London. The first ninety-three were ordered for routes 36, 172, 343 and X68; whilst the other forty-seven were ordered for routes 77, 87 and 171.

The first ninety-three were allocated to London Central. First to arrive were EH171 to EH194 (YY67UPX/Z, URA-C/E-H/J-P/R-X/Z). Arriving earlier than needed in January 2018 they were initially stored in the Crowland area of Lincolnshire before moving to Morden Wharf for further storage. They made another move to their intended garage, New Cross, before the take up of route 343 (New Cross–City Hall) from Abellio London on 3 February 2018. These were joined at New Cross by twenty more in February. They followed on as EH195-214 (YY67USS-X/Z, UTA-C/E-H/J-O) which were ordered against route 172 (Brockley Rise–Clerkenwell Green).

Camberwell received ten E40Hs in March 2018 for use on the X68. These were numbered EH215 to EH224 (YX18KPA/E/F/G/J/K/L/N/O/P) and were used on a number of double-deck routes from Camberwell.

New Cross garage took stock of the final thirty-nine of the initial order. EH225 to EH263 (YX18KYY, KPR/T/U/V/Y/Z, KRD-G/J/K/N/O/U/V/Z, KSE/F/J/K/N/O/U/V/Y/Z, KTA/C-/G/J-L/N/O). This latter fleet of Enviro 400 MMCs were the first of the Ultra-Cap Smart Hybrids to be used by the Go-Ahead London Group, entering service on the 36 (Queens Park – New Cross Gate). EH226 to EH257 and EH260-3 were taken into stock during May 2018, with EH225 and EH258/9 following in June. These were all initially placed into store before entering service.

EH264 to EH284 (SN18KLU/V/X/Z, KMA/E-G/J/K/M/O/U/V/X/Y/Z, KNA-D) were also delivered to the company during April. Allocated to New Cross they were put to use on the 171 (Elephant & Castle–Bellingham, Catford Bus Garage), these being of the standard E40H model.

The order was complete in June when EH285 to EH310 arrived at Stockwell. Registered YX18KWW/Y/Z, KXA-H/J-P/R-W/Y/Z these twenty-six Enviro 400 MMCs were shared between routes 77 (Waterloo–Tooting) and 87 (Wandsworth–Aldwych). These were further ultra-cap models.

Some Enviro 400 MMCs were given all-over advertisements between March 2018 and September 2019. EH55 and EH166 were adorned with advertisements for Michelin in March, both retaining them until June. EH73 was used to promote its green credentials, also carrying the livery between the same dates. EH56 and EH221 were another two MMCs to receive all-over advertisements for Michelin, these being applied in August and being worn until December. In November 2018, EH71 gained an advertisement for TfL's Oyster Hopper, keeping this advertisement until February 2019. It was in February that EH240 was given an advertisement for *Tina; the Musical*. It wore the advertisement until May 2019. The final Enviro 400 MMC to gain an advertisement in this time frame was EH220. It was used to promote 'London is Open', this being a campaign that gave advice to Europeans living in London post-Brexit and their rights to remain in the country. EH220 was later given an all-over advertisement for the Mayor of London, keeping this until November. EH31 had an advertisement for BBC Sounds applied in September 2019. At the same time EH32 received one for the Big Shaq. The latter vehicle retained its advertisement until November 2019, at which time it had another advertisement for Malaysia applied, retaining this one until October 2020.

The final two batches of the standard Enviro 400 MMC double-decker were delivered to Go-Ahead London between June and August 2019, with thirty-three allocated to the Metrobus division. The first seventeen were allocated to Green Street Green for use on the 208 (Lewisham–Orpington, Perry Hall Road). Arriving in June and July they were registered YW19VPC-G/J-P/R/T/U/V/X, taking up rolling stock numbers EH311 to EH327. The other sixteen were delivered in August, following from those used on the 208 as EH328 to EH343. These carried registration marks YW19VVA-H/J-P/R and were allocated to Croydon for route 197 (Peckham Bus Station–Croydon, Katharine Street). EH162 to EH165 were transferred from Camberwell to New Cross in September 2019.

Orders for new double-deckers switched to the Enviro 400EV City bodied BYD D8UR DD in 2020. Forty-nine were initially ordered to cover contracts on routes 106 (Finsbury Park Station-Whitechapel), 212 (Chingford Station–St James Street Station), 230 (Upper Walthamstow–Wood Green) and 357 (Chingford Hatch–Whipp's Cross Hospital). The first thirteen were delivered in February 2020, these being numbered Ee1 to Ee13 (LF20XLA-E/G/H/J-O). Allocated to Northumberland Park these were used on the 212. Eight more followed in March for route 357, these again being allocated to Northumberland Park. These followed on as Ee14-21 (LF20XLP/R/S/T/U/V/W/X). The largest allocation of the forty-nine was used from Northumberland Park on the 106. The route assumed sixteen, Ee22-37 (LF20XLY/Z, XMA-E/G/H/J-/O/P/R). Ee22-30/2 arrived in March, with Ee31/3-7 following in April. The final twelve were again allocated to Northumberland Park when they arrived in June. Ee38 to Ee49 (LF20XNG/J-P/S/T/U) were delivered for use on the 230. However, these were put to use on any of the routes mentioned above.

The next consignment of Ee-class BYDs arrived in April 2021. Twenty were taken into stock for use on route 69 (Walthamstow Central–Canning Town Station). Go-Ahead London opened a new garage further down Factory Road, Silvertown especially for the electric buses. The buses concerned were numbered Ee50 to Ee69 (LG21JFZ, JGF/O/U/V/X/Z, JHA/E/F/H/J-L/O/U/V/X/Z, JJE), these initially being stored at Camberwell.

London Central took stock of eighteen BYD/Enviro 400EV City double-deckers in January and February 2022. Used on the 132 (Bexleyheath–North Greenwich) these buses were numbered EP1 to EP18 (LG71DZH/J-P/R/S-Z, EAA). Whilst these BYDs could be charged in the conventional way, they also had a pantograph fitted as an alternative way of charging. A pantograph was installed at Bexleyheath garage, this causing a problem, with EP1-18 not entering service until July.

**EH166 (YX67VFL)** was one of nine EH-class E40Hs delivered to Camberwell in October 1017. It is photographed on its way to Tottenham Court Road on the 176, having just loaded at the Tenyson Road, Waterloo stop.

**EH179 (YY67URH)** was one of ninety-three E40Hs delivered to Go-Ahead London in 2018 for routes 36, 172, 343 and X68. It is seen passing through Peckham town centre on route 343 to City Hall.

**Another of** the ninety-three EH-class E40Hs that were taken into stock during the first part of 2018 was EH195 (YY67USS). It is seen negotiating Elephant & Castle whilst heading to Waterloo on the 172.

**Sister vehicle,** EH196 (YY67UST), is photographed heading towards Clerkenwell Green on the 172 whilst passing through Waterloo.

**EH212 (YY67UTM)** is also seen on the 343 at Elephant & Castle.

**Route 36 received** the next consignment of Enviro 400 MMCs, these being the first ultra-cap Hybrids to operate with Go-Ahead London. EH229 (YX18KPV) is seen at the Hyde Park Corner end of Park Lane heading towards New Cross Gate.

**EH256 (YX18KTE)** is photographed entering Park Lane having just passed Marble Arch, also heading for New Cross Gate.

**Twenty-one Enviro** 400 MMCs were allocated to route 171 in April 2018. EH281 (SN18KNA) is captured by the camera at the Tennyson Road, Waterloo stops, the bridge carrying the railway line to Waterloo East being seen in the background.

**EH287 (YX18KWZ)** is photographed on the southern side of the River Thames at Lambeth. The Houses of Parliament can be scene at the rear of EH281. The bus was one of twenty-six ultra-cap Smart hybrids used by Go-Ahead London on routes 77 and 87.

**Another of** the twenty-six-strong fleet of EH-class Smart Hybrids delivered for the 77 and 87 is seen entering the town centre area close to Clapham Junction on its way to Waterloo. YX18KXT was given fleet number EH305.

**EH73 (YX66WHR)** was used to promote the 3000 hybrid buses operating in London in August 2019, with a green-based livery being chosen. It is seen on the 363 approaching journeys end at Elephant & Castle.

**EH313 (YW19VPE)** is seen leaving Orpington town centre whilst heading towards Lewisham Station on the 208.

**EH327 (YW19VPX)** is photographed at the other end of the 208 service in Lewisham town centre.

**The final** Enviro 400 MMCs used by Go-Ahead London operated route 197. EH333 (YW19VVF) is photographed in Penge on its way to Croydon town centre.

**2020 saw** the first electric Enviro 400EV City bodied BYD D8UR DD double-deckers taken into stock by Go-Ahead London. Totalling forty-nine, these were shared between routes 106, 212, 230 and 357. The second member of the batch, Ee2 (LF20XLB) is seen in Hackney on its way to Finsbury Park on the 106.

**Ee26 (LF20XMC)** is another of the of the forty-nine BYDs delivered during 2020. The limitations of passenger numbers during the Covid-19 Pandemic can be seen on the entrance doors. It is seen at Walthamstow Central bus station before completing the short journey to St James Street.

**Ee34 (LF20XMM)** is photographed bypassing Walthamstow bus station, passing along the main road close by. It is seen on its way to Whipp's Cross.

**The penultimate** member of the original fleet of Ee-class BYDs (Ee48–LF20XNT) is photographed at the start of its journey to Upper Walthamstow in Wood Green.

**Another twenty** BYD/Enviro 400EV City double-deckers were taken into stock for use on the 69, these being allocated to a new garage in Silvertown. Ee51 (LG21JGF) represents them and is seen on layover at Canning Town Bus Station before heading back to Stratford shortly after being delivered to the company.

**Eighteen BYDs** were taken into stock during 2022 with a pantograph on top for quick charging, these were classified EP by Go-Ahead. EP1 (LG71DZH), is seen at Eltham Church on its way to Bexleyheath.

**The overhead** charging facility mentioned previously is installed at Bexleyheath garage. It is at this location we find EP15 (LG71DZX), seen parked underneath the charger shortly before it being connected.

Route 197 passed from Metrobus to London Central from 18 June 2022. This led to the transfer of EH328-343 from Croydon to Peckham. At the same time EH61 and EH62 transferred from Camberwell to Peckham.

Go-Ahead London lost the 135 to Tower Transit in May 2022. After this date the EHVs were used as spare vehicles. EHV5, 8, 11 and 15 moved from River Road, Barking to Merton to help with problems being experienced on route 200 (Mitcham–Raynes Park), with these also being used on other double-deck routes from Merton. Other members of the type were put to use on school services in the Romford and Ilford areas. After the school term finished in July 2022, they were placed into storage ready for the take up of route 91 (Crouch End–Trafalgar Square) on 4 February 2023. However, EHV14 was used at Peckham for various routes. EHV1, 2, 14 and 16 were temporarily allocated to Stockwell in December 2022 for use one the 77, 87/N87, 88/N88 and 155. EHV5, 8, 9, 11, 15 re-joined the others at Stockwell on the 91 in February 2023.

Twenty-four BYDs arrived in October 2022 with Metrobus. They were allocated to Croydon where they were used on the 119 (Bromley North Station–Purley Way, Colonnades) and 264 (West Croydon Bus Station–Tooting, St Georges Hospital). These took up rolling stock numbers Ee70 to Ee93 (LG72DNO/U/V/X/Y, DOA/H/J/U, DPE/F/K/N/O/U/V/X/Y/Z, DRO/V/X/Z, DSE). These were the first of their type with Go-Ahead London to feature the new LED destination displays, and they entered service in mid-December. The lack of power supply at Croydon led to the transfer of EH226 to EH237 in July and August 2022. They were used on the 264 until the power supply was installed.

To help celebrate the Platinum Jubilee in 2022, several London buses were decorated in a special livery. Ee31 was one of those chosen, wearing the livery between May and September 2022.

Ee43 gained an all-over advertisement for Evian in May, only retaining this for a month, returning to red in June. Ee8 was decorated with an all-over advertisement in December for OVO Energy, with Ee11 being used to promote Lenovo at the same time.

The entry into service of Ee70-93 allowed EH226-37 to move from Croydon to Peckham in January and February 2023. They were used to replace E-class Enviro 400s on the 37 (Peckham–Putney Heath, Green Man) which passed to New Cross, which in turn replaced WVL-class Volvo B9TLs on the 321. EH238 made the move to Peckham from New Cross for the same purpose in February.

Go-Ahead London placed an order for 110 electric buses in May 2022, with seventy-eight of these being of the BYD D8UR DD/Enviro 400EV City double-deckers, these being split between Croydon for the 353 (Ramsden Estate–Forestdale) and Sutton for routes 80 (Hackbridge–Belmont Highdown Prisnon), 93 (Putney Bridge Station–North Cheam), 154 (Morden–West Croydon) and 213 (Kingston–Sutton Bus Garage). The first of these arrived in February numbered Ee101-11 (LD72XZT/U/V/W/X/Y/Z, YAA/E/F/G), Ee113-6 (LG23FFV/W/X/Y), and Ee145-50 (LD72UHT/U/V/W/X/Y). Ee103-111 were originally intended to be allocated to Sutton, but instead were allocated to Metrobus at Green Street Green for use on the 353. The others were allocated, as intended, to Sutton. Between February and April Ee112 (LD72YAH), Ee117-28 (LG23FFZ, FGA/C-F/J/K/M-P), Ee129-144 (LG23FAA/F/J/K/M/O/U, FBA-F/J/K/L), Ee151-62 (LG23FGU/V/X/Z, FHA-F/H/J) and Ee163-71 (LG23EZH/J-P/R). The outstanding vehicles of this order arrived in June, numbered Ee94 to Ee99 (LG23FJD-F/J/K/N). Ee172 to Ee186 were also delivered in June carrying registration marks LG23EUN-P/R/T-Z, EVB-D/F. intended for Sutton they were placed into storage. Ee173-6/9-186 were later allocated to Merton for use on the 57 (Kingston – Clapham Park), taking up service in November. Ee177 and Ee178 found homes at Sutton in August.

Ee35 was given an all-over advertisement in May 2023 for Evian. A month later Ee16 and EP1 were both used to promote OVO Energy. Ee5 and EP13 were two of a number of electric buses in London used to promote the fact that they were Zero Emissions in July. In August, four Ee-class double-deckers received all-over advertisements. Ee154/6/63/9 were used to promote their Zero Emission credentials. Ee8 lost its advertisement for OVO energy, with Ee35 losing its advertisement for Evian.

The next eighteen BYD D8UR DDs arrived with the company in August and September 2023. Following on from those that had been delivered in June, they took up rolling stock numbers Ee187 to Ee204 (LB23PFU/V/X/Y/Z, PGE/F/K/O/U/V/X/Y/Z, PHA/F/J/K), with Ee201-4 (LB23PHA/F/J/K) taking up new registration marks LG73FTJ/K/N/O before entering service. They were allocated to Camberwell where they were initially used on the 40, with some also working the 35. These were joined by Ee172 which had arrived in June. An all-over advertisement celebrating the 75th anniversary of the *Windrush* was applied, with Ee172 being shown off at the Notting Hill Carnival before moving to Camberwell. This livery was retained until July 2024.

TfL introduced a new series of services linking with each, making a number of orbital express routes around the suburbs of Greater London, naming it the Superloop. Some of the other express services already in operation were renumbered and added to the Superloop network. One of these was the X68 (West Croydon–Russell Square). By September this route had been renumbered SL6, with a fleet of Enviro 400 MMCs (EH213-224) being repainted into a white and red livery, carrying branding for the service.

Further Ee-class Enviro 400EV City bodied BYDs were taken into stock at Camberwell during October. Numbered Ee218 to Ee242 (LG73FPV/X/Y/Z, FRC/D/F/J/K/L/N/O/P/R/U/V/X/Z, FSA/C/D/E/F/J/K), they were taken into stock to convert the 185 (Lewisham–Victoria Station) to all-electric. These were shared with route 40, with those ordered against the 40 also seeing service on the 185.

Ee100 put in an appearance in November 2023. Due to the lateness of its arrival, registration mark LG23FJO that had been booked for it was cancelled, being replaced by LG73FTL. This saw service on the 57 from Merton, along with Ee99.

In November, a couple of Enviro 400EV City double-deckers were given all-over advertisements. Ee200 was used to promote the 2023 Poppy Appeal when it was applied in October, retaining it until November. EA6 was the second, being adorned with an advertisement for Bruichladdich. EP13 lost its all-over advertisement for Zero Emissions in December.

Route 91 transferred northwards from Stockwell to Northumberland Park on 20 January 2024. This saw the transfer of EHV2 to EHV16 between the two garages at the same time. EHV1 had transferred to Northumberland Park in December 2023 for use as a type trainer. The EHV-class were then also used on the 476.

The first new Enviro 400 City bodied BYDs for 2024 arrived in March. These were numbered Ee205 to Ee217 (LF24ZJV/X/Y/Z, ZKA/B/C/D/E/G/H/J/K). Allocated to Merton they entered service on the 57 in April. The 57 had been operated by Ee176-189, these latter buses moving to Sutton where they were intended to operate the 151.

Twenty Ee-class Enviro 400EV City buses arrived in March 2024. These were numbered Ee243 to Ee262 and were intended to operate on the 157 (Morden–Crystal

Palace). These carried registration marks LF24ZGC-E/G/H/J-P/R-Y. However, some of these were placed in store either at Morden Wharf or River Road, Barking. Two of this batch were allocated to Bexleyheath. Ee244 and Ee245 entered service wearing a two-tone blue livery and were used to promote gender equality across the bus industry. These saw service on the 132 alongside the EP-class Enviro 400 City double-deckers. The pair were the first buses carrying a 24 registration mark to enter service on a TfL route. A couple of months later, in June, eleven additional Ee-class double-deckers arrived with Go-Ahead London at Merton. Numbered Ee263 to Ee273 (LF24ZNW-Z, ZPB-E/G/H/J), these saw service on the 157. With the transfer of Ee243-262 onto the 157, these buses were moved across to Silvertown, being used on the 262 (Stratford–Galleons Reach).

Ee36 (LF20XMP) and EP1 (LG71DZH) both had their all-over advertisement for OVO Energy replaced by a revised version in February 2024, retaining these until July. In February, Ee154/6, 163/9 lost their advertisements for Zero Emissions. Ee5 lost its all-over advertisement promoting its low emissions in April. EH119 and EH202 gained all-over advertisements for the £5.25 All Day ticket for London in July. Enviro 400 EV City bodied BYD D8UR DD Ee2 was decorated in September 2024 to promote Chilly's. The same month saw EH240 have an all-over advertisement for White Fox applied.

**On 4 February** 2023, Go-Ahead London took up the contract for route 91, with the EHV-class Enviro 400 MMCs moving across to the route from Stockwell. EHV6 (BL15HBJ) is photographed passing Euston fire station whilst heading towards Trafalgar Square.

**In October** 2022, twenty-four Ee-class BYDs were taken into stock by the Metrobus division of Go-Ahead London for routes 119 and 264. Ee73 (LG72DNX) is photographed about to climb the hill towards East Croydon station whilst heading towards Bromley North.

**West Croydon** bus station finds Ee84 (LG72DPU), seen heading to its stands at journeys end on the 264.

**Bromley North** finds Ee92 (LG72DRZ) which is seen on its way to Croydon on the 119. The electric bus branding can be clearly seen above the driver window.

**In the** opening months of 2023, a fleet of Enviro 400 MMCs transferred from Croydon to Peckham for use on the 37, displacing older buses on the route. EH226 (YX18KPR), is captured by the camera crossing the rail lines at Clapham Junction when on its way to Peckham.

**Ee103 to** Ee111 were diverted from Sutton to Croydon garage for the take up of route 353, these being slotted in between batches for Sutton. Ee108 (LD72YAA) is seen leaving Orpington town centre on its way to Forrestdale.

**Route 154 was** one of the Sutton services to be converted to the Ee-Class BYDs. Ee120 (LG23FGD) is photographed loading in Sutton town centre on its way to West Croydon. One disadvantage to these new buses is that the destination displays rarely come out in photographs.

**Route 93 was** another route operated from Sutton; this being converted to the Ee-class. Ee124 (LG23FGK) is photographed at Wimbledon bus station.

**Sutton finds** Ee138 (LG23FBC) whilst on its way to Belmont on route 80.

**Route 213 links** Sutton with Kingston upon Thames. Ee156 (LG23FHB) is seen on its way to the latter destination whilst passing through Sutton town centre.

**Ee179 (LG23EUW)** was one of the BYDs used to convert route 57 to the type in November 2022. It is seen in Kingston whilst heading towards Clapham Park.

**The summer** of 2023 saw the arrival of eighteen BYD Ee-class double-deckers at Camberwell to start the conversion of routes 40 and 35. Ee191 (LB23PFZ) is found at Camberwell whilst operating the 40.

**Ee197 (LB23PGV)** is seen heading the other way through Camberwell Green whilst operating a journey on the 35.

**Ee172 (LG23EUN)** was to have been allocated to Merton for use on the 57. However, it was reallocated to Camberwell where it was used on the 35, 40 and 185. It received an all-over advertisement celebrating the *Windrush* generation before entering service. It seen passing through Camberwell carrying this livery.

**The next** batch of Ee-class BYDs were also allocated to Camberwell, these being delivered to convert the 185 to all-electric. Ee223 (LG73FRD) is another of the type captured by the camera at Camberwell. It is seen heading towards Lewisham Station, with another of the type seen to the right of the photograph.

**Ee235 (LG73FRZ)** is another of the fleet of Ee-class double-decks taken into stock at Camberwell for the 185. However, it is seen operating route 40 to Elephant & Castle instead of a its intended route. The Ee-class allocated to Camberwell for routes 35, 40 and 185 are used indiscriminately on all three routes.

**Route 91 transferred** from Stockwell to Northumberland Park, with the EHV-class moving with the route, with the type also used on the 476, as shown by EHV10 (BL15HBX). It is seen passing under the platforms at St Pancras International, travelling to its first stop after its layover at King's Cross, although the blind has yet to be reset.

**Ee244 (LF24ZGO)** arrived in March 2024. It was one of two of the type to receive a two-tone blue livery to promote gender equality within the bus industry. It is seen on layover at Green Street Green garage. *Rob Waughman*

**Ee264 (LF24ZNX)** is photographed about to depart Stratford bus station at the start of its journey to Galleons Reach on the 262.

# TOWER TRANSIT

**Tower Transit** only operated three Enviro 400 MMCs. The first of these, DH38501 (SN65ZGO), is seen departing Walthamstow bus station on the 69, the route that all three were employed on. It can be seen carrying the green-leaf livery applied to the early generation of hybrid buses.

Tower Transit operated just three Enviro 400 MMC buses. It had been intended that four electric Enviro 400 MMCs were to have been operated on route 69 by Stagecoach London. However, the 69 passed to Tower Transit in 2016, with these buses transferring across to the latter operator. Induction plates were installed at both Walthamstow and Canning Town bus stations.

Three Enviro 400 MMC VE (virtual electric) arrived in the latter months of 2015. The first, DH38501 (SN65ZGO), arrived in October, with the other two being delivered in November and December, following on as DH38502 and DH38503 (SN65ZGP/R). They were operated by Tower Transit, paralleling workings operated by Stagecoach London until the route was officially taken over by Tower Transit. They were allocated to Lea Interchange garage and wore the 'green leaf' livery.

These were withdrawn by Tower Transit and sold in November 2021, appearing with Uno Buses of Hatfield in 2023 for use on London area school routes.

# ARRIVA LONDON

Arriva London were the first to take stock of the Enviro 400 City based on the hybrid E40H chassis. Nineteen arrived at the end of 2015, beginning of 2016 for use on the 78 (Shoreditch-Nunhead), operating from Ash Grove garage. HA1 to HA7 (LK65BYX/Y/Z, BZA/B/C/D) entered the Arriva London fleet in November 2015. These were followed by HA8-15/7/8 (LK65BZE-G, BYM-P/R, BYT/U) in December. HA16 and HA19 (LK65BYS/V) completed delivery in January 2016. All had entered service by the end of January 2016. Demonstrator SN65OHP was loaned to the company from Alexander Dennis in November, and was used by the company as a type trainer, returning off loan in February 2016.

Route 133 (Liverpool Street–Streatham Station) also received some Enviro 400 City bodied E40H at the end of 2016. They continued the fleet numbering sequence as HA20 to HA53 (LK66GZM-P/S-W/Y, HAE/O/X, HBA-H/J/L/N-P/U/X-Z, HCA/C-E). HA20-9 were delivered to the company in November, with the others following in December. The 133 was operated from Arriva London South's garage at Brixton.

The annual Poppy Appeal livery was applied to Arriva London's HA19 in October 2018, this being removed in December.

Twenty-eight Smart Hybrid Enviro 400 MMC double-decks were ordered by Arriva London for delivery during 2020. Upon arrival these buses were numbered HT1 to HT28 by the company, taking up registration marks SK20BFY/Z, BGE/F/O/U/V/X/Y/Z, BHA, SK70BUU, BUV, BE, BUW, BVF/A/N/B/C/J/O/L/D/P/G/H/M. HT1-4 arrived in August, with the others putting in an appearance in September. Norwood took stock of HT1-17 and HT20, whilst South Croydon were allocated HT18/9, 21-8, with HT20 moving from Norwood to South Croydon in October 2020. Those at Norwood were used on route 202 (Crystal Palace–Blackheath, Royal Standard), whilst those at South Croydon operated the 405 (Croydon - Redhill).

Another twenty-two Enviro 400 City double-decks were purchased by Arriva London in 2021, this time being allocated to Brixton for use on the 319 (Sloane Square–Brixton Garage). These were numbered EA1 to EA22 (LG71DJK/O/U/V/X/Y/Z, DKA/D/E/F/J/K/L/N/O/U/V/X/Y, DLD/E. Delivery of these was drawn out, with EA1-3 arriving in August; EA4-13 in September; EA14-21 in October and EA22 arriving in November. Demonstrator LF69UXJ was loaned to Brixton in September for use as a type trainer.

Thornton Heath were allocated twelve of the Enviro 400 City double-deckers for use on route 198 (Thornton Heath–Shrublands) in February 2022. HA20-6/8-31 made the move from Brixton at this time, being joined by HA27, which came via Ash Grove. The peak vehicle requirement for the route was twelve. This led to the transfer of HA19 from Ash Grove in August.

EA5 (LG71DJX) lost its original registration mark in February in favour of cherished registration mark 185CLT. A couple of months later, in May, EA1 was decorated to celebrate the Platinum Jubilee, retaining this until September, while EA21 received an all-over advertisement for Evian Water, losing this in June. Another two EAs had all-over advertisements applied to them in December. EA11 was used to promote Lenovo, whilst EA22 was given an advertisement for OVO Energy, retaining this livery until January 2024.

Three more EAs were adorned with all-over advertisements during 2023. EA12 was used to promote the toilet tissue brand 'Who Gives a Crap' in April. This was followed in May by EA2 which was another of the type used to promote Evian Water. The pair lost these advertisements in August and September 2023 respectively. The final member of the type to receive an advertisement during the year was EA2 which was used to promote OVO Energy.

As mentioned under the Go-Ahead London chapter, a new network of orbital services, with some splinter routes, was introduced in the latter part of 2023 under the Superloop brand. Fourteen Enviro 400 City double-deckers, HA1-14, which had become spare from the loss of the 78, were allocated to the new SL1 service linking North Finchley and Walthamstow Central, this commencing operation on 2 December 2023. By the time the route had started, HA2-14 had been repainted red and white, and branded for the service.

Following the loss of the 133 and 333 in January 2024, HA36-40/2-53 had become surplus to requirements. Initially being placed in store at Barking, they were soon put to further use on Super Loop service SL2 (Walthamstow Central–North Woolwich). HA36-43/5-53 were given Superloop livery and branding.

EA3 was adorned with a revised version of the OVO Energy livery in February 2024, replacing a similar livery already worn by this bus. EA11 lost its advertisement for Lenovo in March 2024, adorning a new advertisement for McCains at the same time. EA11 lost this advertisement in June.

Enviro 400 City double-deckers HA15/6/8, 32-5 transferred in March to Norwood garage where they were put in a generic vehicle pool that were used on rail replacement work. HA17 was allocated to Barking in August, this being used as a spare bus for the Superloop SL2 service.

**Arriva London** first took stock of the Enviro 400 City in late 2015 for route 78. The first of these numerically was HA1 (LK65BYX) which is seen loading in Peckham town centre whilst heading towards Shoreditch.

**Another of** the route 78 fleet of Enviro 400 City buses is HA5 (LK65BZB). It is seen loading at the Dunton Road/ Old Kent Road stop, the latter road can be glimpsed in the background.

**The City** of London provides the backdrop to this photograph of HA22 (LK66GZO) which is seen having just crossed London Bridge on its way to Streatham Station.

**HA50 (LK66HCA)** is seen heading towards Liverpool Street whilst passing through Elephant & Castle.

**Arriva London** purchased twenty-eight Enviro 400 MMCs in 2020. Seventeen of these were allocated to Norwood for use on the 202. HT1 (SK20BFY) is photographed entering a wet Crystal Palace bus station.

**The other** HT-class Enviro 400 MMCs were allocated to South Croydon. They were used on the 405 between Croydon and Redhill. Captured by the camera in Croydon town centre, HT23 (SK70BVL) is seen on its way to Redhill.

**EA5 was** originally registered LG71DJX when delivered to Arriva London. In February 2022 it was given cherished registration mark 185CLT which it is seen carrying as it passes through Streatham on its way to Streatham Hill, Telford Avenue.

**EA12 (LG71DKJ)** is photographed passing through Clapham Junction town centre whilst heading towards Sloane Square and in April 2023 an all-over advertisement for the toilet roll brand 'Who Gives a Crap?' was applied.

**Arriva London** operated two of the Superloop services, the first of these being the SL1 between Walthamstow Central and North Finchley. HA012 (LK65BYN) is seen departing Walthamstow Central on its way to the latter destination.

**The second** of the Superloop services links Walthamstow Central with the North Woolwich Ferry Terminal. Both routes carry the red and white Superloop livery, with the buses also carrying appropriate route branding for the two services. HA52 (LK66HCD) is also seen departing Walthamstow Central.

# HACKNEY COMMUNITY TRANSPORT (CT PLUS)

Hackney Community Transport, trading as CT Plus, did not purchase any standard Enviro 400 MMC, instead they opted for the Enviro 400 City.

The first twenty-one arrived in June 2016 for use on the 26 (Hackney Wick–Waterloo). Allocated to Ash Grove they were numbered 2501 to 2521 (SN16OHP/R-Z, OJA-H/J/K/L). They wore an all-red livery relieved only by small CT Plus logos. Prior to their arrival, demonstrator SN65OHP was loaned during May. 2510 suffered fire damage in October 2016 and needed to go away for repair. As mentioned under the Demonstrator chapter earlier in this book, its place was taken by Enviro 400 MMC demonstrator YY64GXG. 2510 returned to service in January 2017.

Hackney Community Transport had been operating the 388 (Stratford City–Blackfriars) from Ash Grove since the route was introduced in January 2003. The rolling stock used on the route was upgraded in 2017 with sixteen new Enviro 400 City double-deckers. Numbered 2522 to 2537 (SN66WRE/G/J/K/L/O/P/R/T/U/V/W/X/Z, WSD/E), these arrived in January (2522-8), February (2529-35/7) and March (2536). Seventeen of the type had been originally ordered, but was reduced by one following the acquisition of the former demonstrator SN65OHP, this operating with the company as 2538. It was acquired from Alexander Dennis in February 2017. These displaced the unique fleet of Transbus Trident bodied East Lancs Myllennium double-decks on the route.

CT Plus won the contract for route 20 (Debden–Walthamstow Central) in March 2019. Nine additional Enviro 400 City bodied E40H were purchased to take up service on the route, being allocated to Walthamstow Stadium. These were numbered 2539 to 2547 (YX19ORO/P/S/T/U/V/W/Y/Z). Two additional buses were required for the route, these being made up by the transfer of 2537 and 2538 from Ash Grove following a reduction in the pvr on the 388.

The final standard Enviro 400 Citys to arrive with CT Plus arrived in October 2019. 2548 and 2549 (YX69NLY/Z) were allocated to Ash Grove to provide extra cover on the 26 and 388 as required. Both vehicles transferred to Walthamstow in October and November 2019 respectively.

Enviro 400EV City bodied BYD D8UR DD demonstrator LJ69UXJ was loaned twice to CT Plus, the first time being in December 2019, returning to the company in June 2020. This vehicle was used by CT Plus for a third time between March and April 2021.

CT Plus got its own pair of Enviro 400EV City bodied BYD D8UR DD double-deckers in March 2021. 2550e and 2551e (LG21HZM/N) were ordered against the renewal of school route 616. They were also used on the 20 alongside the hybrid Enviro 400 Citys mentioned above.

As mentioned under the Stagecoach London heading, control of Hackney Community Transport passed to the Stagecoach Group on 27 August 2022 leading to the transfer of 158 buses. Just for completeness, 2501-49 and 2550e and 2551e were included in the sale, becoming 12501-49 and 14173/4.

**CT Plus** (Hackney Community Transport) gained the contract for the 26 from Stagecoach London in June 2016. For this twenty Enviro 400 City bodied AD E40Hs were taken into stock. 2505 (SN16OHU) was one of these buses and is seen at the Aldwych just before starting its journey across Waterloo Bridge to its terminus at Waterloo.

**2514 (SN16OJD)** is seen starting its journey northwards to Hackney Wick whilst negotiating the roundabout that surrounds the Imax Cinema at Waterloo. CT Plus applied small fleet names to their buses as can be seen on 2514 above the entrance door.

**Sixteen Enviro** 400 City double-deckers replaced the fleet of East Lancs Myllennium bodied Transbus Tridents, and other double-deck types on the 388 in early 2017. 2526 (SN66WRL) is seen leaving Bishopsgate on its way to Stratford City.

**CT Plus** also helped out on rail replacement work taking their buses to unfamiliar parts of London. This is the case with 2536 (SN66WSD) which is seen crossing Putney Bridge whilst heading towards Wimbledon.

**February 2017** saw the acquisition of former ADL Demonstrator SN65OHP. Upon entering the CT Plus fleet, it was allotted rolling stock number 2538. It is photographed heading towards Stratford City on the 388 at Elephant & Castle.

**Route 20 was** a third service to be converted to the Enviro 400 City by CT Plus, this taking place in 2019. 2543 (YX19ORU) is seen entering Walthamstow bus station.

**In October** 2019 two additional Enviro 400 City buses entered the CT Plus fleet to cover an increase in requirements on the 26 and 388. 2548 was one of the pair and is seen departing Walthamstow Central on the 20 to Debden. Originally registered YX69NLY, it was soon re-registered in E17HCT.

# SULLIVAN BUSES

South Mimms-based Sullivan Buses won the contract for the 217 (Waltham Cross–Turnpike Lane Station) from Metroline, this starting on 3 June 2017. For the route twelve standard Enviro 400 MMC bodied E40Ds were purchased. These took fleet numbers E70 to E81 and carried private registration marks that reflected the initials of members of staff at the company. These were AD, AW, BW, JC, JS, PB, RC, RM, RS, RT, SG, WG17SUL. E70/2-5/7 arrived in April, with the outstanding buses arriving in May. A basic red livery with no fleet names was worn by these buses. Little of interest took place with these buses whilst operating the route.

Sullivan Buses withdrew from TfL work in August 2024. Route 217 was taken over by Arriva London, being operated from Tottenham garage, with support from Palmers Green and Wood Green.

**A small** fleet of Enviro 400 MMCs were operated by Sullivan Buses of South Mimms on the 217. E74 (JS17SUL) is seen approaching the end of its journey at Turnpike Lane, already blinded for its return journey.

# RATP LONDON

RATP London did not take stock of the Enviro 400 MMC until 2018. Four E40H models were received in February for use on the 258 (Watford Junction–South Harrow Station). They took fleet numbers ADH45258 to ADH45261 (YY67UUO/P/R/S) and were allocated to the London Sovereign fleet based at Edgware. Arriving early they were initially stored at Hounslow Heath. The remainder of the order for the 258 did not arrive until the autumn. ADH45278-88 (YX68UNH/J/K/L/M/N/P/S/U/V/W) were delivered in September, with ADH45289-97 (YX68UOJ/K/L/M/N/O/P/R/S) following in October. These were examples of the E40H ultra-cap model. These were the only Enviro 400 MMCs to be purchased by RATP. The gap in fleet numbers between the February and September deliveries were allocated to a fleet of Wrightbus Eclipse Gemini 3 bodied Volvo B5LHs.

**The RATP** London Group operated a small number of Enviro 400 MMCs through their London Sovereign division. ADH45261 (YY67UUS) is seen at the South Harrow terminus of route 258 before setting off back to Watford Junction.

Focus in 2019 turned towards electric buses, with RATPs new double-deck needs being catered for by the Enviro 400EV City bodied BYD D8UR DD. Twenty-nine of these buses were ordered against the contract renewal for the 94 (Acton–Piccadilly Circus). The first of these arrived in December 2019 numbered BCE47001-8, originally to have been BC47001-8. Registration marks LB69JNJ/K/L/N/O/U/V/X were carried. Allocated to London United's Shepherd's Bush garage, BCE47003 was the first of the type to enter service. BCE47009-29 (LB69JNZ, JOA/H/J/UV, JPF/J/O/U/V/X/Y, JRO/U/V/X/Z, JSU/V/X) arrived in the opening months of 2020, with BCE47009-23/5 arriving in January, followed by BCE47024/6-9 in February.

The Enviro 400EV City demonstrator LJ69UXJ was loaned to RATP London in September 2020, being used for trials on the 71 before entering official service on 12 October 2020. During the month it was also used on the 281. It was, however, officially stood down by the end of October, but saw service until mid-November. Allocated to Fulwell for its stay, it was allotted rolling stock number BCE47000 for the duration of its stay.

The fleet of BCE-class BYDs that were used on the 94 were used to promote a number of different companies and products as will be seen during this chapter. BCE47013 was the first of these, being given an all-over advertisement for Courtney Black in March 2021, retaining it until July.

Over the course of 2021 and 2022 no less than 148 Enviro 400EV City bodied BYD D8UR DDs were taken into stock by RATP London, these being delivered out of sequence. However, the allocation and delivery of these buses was quite complex. The lack of electric charging infrastructure at some garages, especially Harrow and Edgware, meant that the allocation of buses was not what had been intended.

The first six of an order of twenty-two for route 281 (Hounslow–Tolworth Broadway) arrived in the summer months of 2021, allocated to Fulwell. Registered LE21FRU/V/X/Z, FSA/C these followed on from the fleet used on route 94, taking stock numbers BCE47030 to BCE47035. BCE47030 arrived in June, the other five in July and were placed into store. BCE47030 was re-registered LG71DVM, whilst BCE47035 became LG71DVN. BCE47036-40 (LE21FSD/F/G/J/K), BCE47044 (LE21FSP) and BCE47084-6 (LE21FTF/J/K) arrived in August, with BCE47040 being allocated to Shepherds Bush in September. They were joined in September by BCE47041/2/3/5/7 (LG71DVO/P/R/T/V) and BCE47093/5/8 (LG71DWK/M/P). BCE47046/8-53 (LG71DVU/W/X/Y/Z, DSX/Y) all arrived in September. Of the new arrivals, BCE47035/93/5 were allocated to Shepherds Bush in October, with BCE47098 finding a home at Fulwell. By October, BCE47087 had been allocated to Shepherds Bush for use on routes 94 and 148 (White City–Camberwell Green). At the same time, BCE47033 was allocated to London Sovereign's Harrow garage for new route X140 (Harrow–Heathrow Central)

A further twenty-one BYDs arrived in October. Numbered BCE47087-93/4/6/7/9-110 (LG71DWA/C-F/J/L/N/O/U, DUU/V/Y, DVA-C/F/H/J-L). Another thirty entered the London United fleet in November. These deliveries helped to fill the gap in the fleet numbering sequence, becoming BCE47054-83 (LG71DXS-Z, DYA-D/F/H/J/M-P/T-Y, DZA/B/C/E/F), with the majority of these being placed into store. BCE47084 to BCE47099 were ear-marked to convert route 49 (White City–Clapham Junction) to the type, these joining the original fleet of BCEs at Shepherds Bush. This, however, did not happen in practice.

BCE47001 was used by RATP London to promote the 2021 Poppy Appeal, carrying the appropriate Poppy livery between October and November 2021. Sister vehicle BCE47002 was used to promote FFI in November 2021, retaining this until January 2022.

2022 opened with the transfer of BCE47033 from Harrow to Fulwell, with BCE47098 making the move in the opposite direction. In the same month BCE47063/89/91/8/100/1/2/5/6/7 were all allocated to Harrow. BCE47042 and BCE47081 were both allocated to Fulwell in February, with BCE47096/9 joining the allocation at Harrow the same month.

BCE47030/41/9/51/5/6/7/8/60/6/8/9/70/2/3/6/9/88/90/2/4/109 were allocated in February to Harrow; whilst BCE47043/5/6/7/8/50/2/3/9/61/2/4/5/7 were further BYDs allocated to Fulwell. BCE47034/5 made the move between Shepherds Bush and Fulwell in March; whilst BCE47030/41/51 transferred to Fulwell from Harrow. At the same time BCE47097 and 47156 were allocated to Fulwell in March. Harrow took stock of BCE47111-3 during March.

**RATP London** took stock of a large number of the BYD D8UR DD/Enviro 400EV City combination for various services. The first twenty-nine were allocated to Shepherds Bush for use on the 94. BCE47001 (LB69JNJ) is seen rounding Marble Arch on its way to Acton Green.

**The fleet** of BCE-class BYDs used on the 94 had a number of all-over advertisements applied to them. BCE47007 (LB69JNV) gained a green-based livery, minus the front, to advertise OVO Energy. It is seen at Shepherds Bush on its way to Acton Green.

**A number** of the BCE-class were used to promote Chiquita Bananas in 2022. One of those used was BCE47014 (LB69JOV), which is seen at Shepherds Bush.

**BCE47037 (LE21FSF)** was delivered to RATP London in August 2021. It is seen operating route 281 to Tolworth whilst passing through Twickenham town centre.

**The early** allocation of the BCE-class was scattered around the RATP London Group. BCE47058 (LG71DXW) was originally allocated to Harrow in February 2022, remaining there until June 2022 when it moved to Fulwell. BCE47058 is seen passing Harrow bus station on its way to Pinner whilst operating the 183.

**Cromwell Road,** Kingston finds BCE47061 (LG71DXZ) operating a journey on the 371, this traditionally being a single-deck service. Kingston became a hot spot for the BCE-class, with routes 65 and 281 operating a large number of the type.

**The 281** also passed through Twickenham town centre between Hounslow and Tolworth. It is this location that BCE47067 (LG71DYH) was captured by the camera whilst heading towards the latter destination.

**Richmond bus** station finds BCE47072 (LG71DYP). It is seen heading towards Kingston.

**BCE47079 (LG71DZA)** is also seen at Harrow just before entering the bus station. It is seen having completed a journey on the X140 from Heathrow Airport, this route now being Super Loop service SL9.

**The 295** was allocated the final batch of BCEs to enter service with RATP London. The route also used other members of the type. This is shown by BCE47084 (LE21FTF), which is seen at Clapham Junction shortly before completing the last leg of its journey.

**Shepherd's Bush** route 49 received a small fleet of BCE-class BYDs in 2022. The top end of Clapham Junction town centre finds BCE47098 (LG71DWP), heading towards White City on the 49.

**BCE47125 (LG22AUP)** was originally ordered for route 125. However, they were soon reallocated to Harrow for use on the 183. It is seen at Harrow bus station showing off the 'I am an electric bus' branding.

**BCE47137 (LG22AVF)** was also allocated to Harrow for use on the X140 service linking Heathrow Airport and Harrow. It is photographed at Heathrow Central bus station having just arrived from Harrow.

Two further batches of BCE-class Enviro 400EV City double-deckers were delivered to RATP London between February and May. BCE47138-56 (LG71DWV/W/X/Y/Z, DXA/B/C/D/E/F/H/J/K/L/M/O/P/R) arrived in February. These had been earmarked for route 125 operating from Edgware. However, these were reallocated to Fulwell. BCE47111-137 (LG22ATZ/Y/Z, AUA/C/E/F/H/J/K/L/M/N/O/P/R/T/U/V/W/X/Y, AVB/C/D/E/F) arrived between March and May 2022. These were allocated to Harrow where they were used on the 183 (Golders Green–Pinner).

Further BCEs were allocated to Fulwell in June, with BCE47040/4 moving from Shepherds Bush. BCE47055-8/63/6/8/9/73/6/9 transferred in from Harrow. BCE47139-47/9/50/1 moved into Harrow from Fulwell. Shepherds Bush based BCE47084/6/9 transferred to Westbourne Park in October. The former garage being allocated BCE47129 in September. Sister vehicles, BCE47131-7, were placed into store at Westbourne Park for a while in June. Further allocation of BCEs to Harrow in October saw BCE47126-8/30/1/3-7 enter service from this garage.

The power supply at Edgware garage was finally switched on at the end of October. This led to the transfer of BCEs into the garage in October and November to take up service on the 125. BCE47138-42/4/5/7-51 transferred from Harrow in October, whilst BCE47148/52-6 transferred from Fulwell in November. BCE47087 also moved into Edgware from Shepherds Bush. BCE47085 and BCE47129 which were also allocated to Shepherds Bush, were both re-allocated to Westbourne Park and Harrow respectively.

BCE47070 (LG71DYN) was decorated in a commemorative livery for the 2022 Jubilee, also being re-registered ER70LXX in April 2022, keeping this registration mark until September.

Fifteen BCEs were adorned with all-over advertisements during 2022. The first three were completed in March. BCE47003 was used to promote Ami during the month, this being the first of three advertisements carried by this bus in 2022. BCE47007 and BCE47025 were used to promote OVO Energy at the same time. BCE47006 was used to promote Evian water in May. A second advertisement was applied to BCE47003 in June when it was used to promote Marc Jacobs, as was BCE47005. They both retained this livery until July, when they were both adorned with advertisements for Chiquita Bananas. They were joined in July by BCE47013/4/22 which had similar advertisements applied. BCE47016 was another of the type to have more than one advertisement applied during the year. This latter bus lost its advertisement in March. In August it had an advertisement for Qatar applied, this being replaced by one for Codornui in October. An advertisement for San Pellegrino was applied to BCE47009 in September. BCE47022 was the bus chosen to promote the 2022 Poppy Appeal, wearing the livery between October and November. The final three were decorated with all-over advertisements in December. BCE47026 gained one for Lenovo; whilst BCE47031 and BCE47120 were used to promote OVO Energy, losing this in April 2024.

The final BCEs to be taken into stock by RATP London arrived in December 2022. These followed on as BCE47157-77 (LG72EEA/B/F, LD72UFV-Z, UGA-C/E-G/J-P). BCE47161 was originally allocated to Harrow and BCE47162-4 to Fulwell. The others were placed into store at Westbourne Park before entering service on the 295 (Clapham Junction–Ladbrooke Grove Sainsbury's). BCE47161 was also briefly allocated to Shepherds Bush. Over the course of February and March 2023, BCE47087/90/1 were also transferred to Westbourne Park for the take up of the 295. BCE47088 and BCE47092 joined them in May.

Ten BCE-class double-deckers were used to promote various products during 2023. BCE47007 was the first to be completed in March, being another of the type to promote

OVO Energy. The next two were done during April; BCE47014 being used to promote Evian water, whilst BCE47016 was adorned with an advertisement for the 'Who Gives a Crap' toilet tissue. June was a busy month for the application of advertisements. BCE47008/19/21 all received advertisements for Chiquita Bananas, whilst BCE47013 and BCE47091 were both used to promote OVO Energy, this being retained until March 2024. BCE47066 was another example used to promote OVO Energy in July. At the same time, BCE47031 was adorned with an advertisement to promote the Zero Emission credentials. BCE47013 lost its OVO Energy advertisement in July, this being replaced by one for Chiquita Bananas Mosaic. This was replaced again in September, with BCE47013 regaining an advertisement for OVO Energy. BCE47008 lost its Chiquita Bananas advertisement in October in favour of one for the 2023 Poppy Appeal, retaining this until December. The final BCEs to gain all-over advertisements did so in November. BCE47017 was used to promote the Women in Bus & Coach campaign. BCE47019 lost its Chiquita Bananas advertisement in favour of one for Bruichladdich.

Superloop route SL10 (Harrow–North Finchley) was introduced on 25 November 2023. Harrow based BCE47087-92, 47111-9 were used on the service, with BCE47087-90/2/111-9 being repainted into the red and white Superloop livery, complete with route branding. They were joined by a second route SL9 Which replaced the former express service X140 (Heathrow Airport–Harrow). For this, BCE47084-6/100-10 were also decorated in Superloop livery.

BCE47014 and BCE47021 lost their advertisements for Chiquita Bananas in January 2024, with BCE47008 and BCE47168 was given all-over advertisements for Zidag and Voltaire

**Cromwell Road** bus station provides the backdrop to this photograph of BCE47155 (LG71DXP). It is seen loading before continuing its journey to Tolworth on the 281.

in February and BCE47008 losing this livery in May. BCE47168 wore this livery for longer, eventually losing it in July 2024. BCE47013 and BCE47066 received a revised version of the OVO Energy all-over advertisement in February, as did BCE47167. Both buses retained this livery until July 2024 when they were returned to red livery. BCE47013 lost its OVO Energy advertisement in June, it being replaced by one for Chiquita Bananas.

RATP London were allocated two of the Superloop services, both meeting in Harrow. A fleet of BCE-class Enviro 400 EV City bodied BYDs were used on the routes. BCE47084-6/100-10 were used on the SL9 between Heathrow Airport and Harrow, with these buses receiving Superloop livery and branding for the service. BCE47087-90/2/111-9 were put to use on the SL10 (Harrow to North Finchley). BCE47087-90/2/111-9 were decorated in the Superloop livery and branding for the SL10.

A handful of the BCE-class buses were decorated with all-over advertisements during 2024. BCE47019 lost its advertisement for Bruichladdich in favour of one for the Love Philippines campaign in March which it kept until May. The same month saw BCE47027 gain an advertisement for McCains, wearing this livery until May and in July, BCE47010 and BCE47028 were used to promote the *Despicable Me 4* film. The latter double-decker lost this advertisement in September. Another two BCE-class double-deckers had all-over advertisements applied during August. At this time BCE47007 was used to promote its Zero Emissions credentials; whilst BCE47025 was used to promote tourism to Thailand. September 2024 saw all-over advertisements applied to three BCE-class BYDs. BCE47011 was used to promote White Fox. BCE47013 lost its advertisement for Chiquita Bananas but was adorned with another promoting San Miguel. An advertisement for Chilly's was applied to BCE47015.

**BCE47177 (LD72UGP)** is the last of the BCE-class to be operated by the RATP London Group. It is seen crossing the bridge over the rail lines at Clapham Junction, heading towards Ladbrooke Grove Sainsburys on the 295.

**In October** 2022 BCE47022 (LB69JRO) was decorated for the 2022 Poppy Appeal. It is seen passing through Notting Hill Gate on its way to Piccadilly Circus on the 94 wearing this livery.

**RATP Group** operate two of the Super Loop services, these meeting each other at Harrow. The former X140 service was renumbered SL9. BCE47101 (LG71DUV) is seen having just loaded at the stop outside Hayes & Harlington station wearing the Super Loop livery, complete with appropriate route branding.

# OTHER ENVIRO 400 MMCs

## Reading Buses

Reading Buses took over operation of the Green Line services 702 (London Victoria–Windsor–Bracknell) and 703 (Bracknell–Heathrow Airport) from First Berkshire on 27 December 2017. The route was initially operated by various types of buses and coaches. These included a pair of Enviro 400 MMCs registered YX64VRU and YY15OYA, these being numbered 758 and 759 by Reading Buses. Sister vehicle 757 (YX64VRT) was also used on the 702 in May 2018. This latter double-decker wore a purple and gold livery commemorating the marriage of Prince Harry and Meghan Markle. These three double-deckers were used on the route alongside Scania single-deckers. In June 2019, 757 lost the Royal Wedding livery in favour of the two-tone grey livery worn by 758 and 759.

A pair of Enviro 400 MMC demonstrators were loaned to the company in January 2018, these both being used on the 702. The first was based on a Scania N250UD chassis, this being allotted temporary fleet number 778 (YN16CFU). The second was a

**758 (YX64VRU)** was one of two Enviro 400 MMCs were originally used on the 702 service between Victoria and Bracknell when Reading Buses took over the route from First Berkshire in 2017. It is seen at Victoria wearing a celebratory livery for the Coronation of His Royal Highness King Charles III.

standard E40D model. This followed on as 779 (YX67UZB). A third Enviro 400 MMC demonstrator came on loan to Reading Transport in September, this again being used on the 702. Numbered 106, this bus carried registration mark DD16GAS. 106 carried a Scania N280UD chassis and was powered by gas.

Reading Transport ordered five Optare MetroDeckers for use on the 702 to help standardise the fleet used on the route in 2019. However, the order for these buses was later cancelled.

The fleet of Enviro 400 MMCs used on the Green Line services were changed in March 2020. 756 and 757 mentioned above were taken off these routes, being used on Reading area services. 760 to 762 (YY15OKB-D) were used to replace them. The trio wore a green livery from their time on Reading area services 5 and 6. It was at this time that the Enviro 400/Enviro 400 MMC became the standard type on the Green Line services.

Enviro 400 MMC 795 (SN66WLK) was repainted into Green Line livery in August 2021. This bus had been previously used on contract work in the Didcot area by the Thames Valley subsidiary of Reading Buses. In February 2022, another Enviro 400 MMC was repainted into Green Line livery. 781 (SN66WRC) had been used by the Thames Valley Buses operation on a Vodafone contract. By April 2022, 758 received a livery to celebrate the Platinum Jubilee. A couple of months later, in July, 781 and 782 (SN66WRC and SN66WRD) gained a two-tone green livery. They were initially given Green Line branding, before later being branded as Flightline, these being used on route 703.

Seven Enviro 400 City double-deckers were delivered to Reading Transport over the summer of 2023. These were numbered 731 to 737 (RG23BUS, GL23SLH, GL23WND, GL23LGO, GL23BKL and GL23LHR). 732 was first to arrive in June, followed by 731/3-7 in July. The last three letters of the registration mark represents a location served by the route. A generic grey livery was worn by 731, with a two-tone green livery applied to 732-7; with 732 to 735 branded for the London Line 702 service, and 736 and 737 having branding for the Flightline 703 service.

**In July** 2021, 781 (SN66WRC) gained the two-tone livery for the Green Line service between Heathrow and Slough. It is seen heading towards the latter destination when leaving Heathrow Terminal 5.

**RG23BUS was** numerically the first of seven Enviro 400 City double-decks taken into stock by Reading Buses during the summer of 2023. Numbered 731, it wore a two-tone grey livery as seen above, becoming a spare vehicle for the 702 and 703. It is seen at Victoria whilst operating the 702.

**Three other** Enviro 400 City double-deckers were taken into stock for use on the London to Slough service. 732 (GL23LDN) was one of these buses and is seen at Victoria wearing the two-tone livery applied to these buses, along with the route branding.

**Two additional** Enviro 400 City buses were taken into stock and put to use on the Flightline 703 service. 736 (GL23LHR) was the first of the pair and is seen leaving Slough town centre on its way to Heathrow Terminal 5.

**Reading Buses** used other Enviro 400 MMCs as required on their 702 and 703 services. Emerald route branded 768 (YY15OYK) is captured by the camera at Hyde Park Corner shortly before reaching the terminus at Victoria.

760-2 (YY15OYB-D) were branded for Flightline services 730 (Frimley–Camberley–Bagshot–Heathrow Airport) and 731 which linked Basingstoke with Frimley. The trio were allocated to the Newbury & District division of Reading Transport. During December 2023, a similar number of Plaxton Panther bodied Volvo B8R coaches were purchased by Reading Transport, replacing 760-2 on these services.

Three hi-specification Enviro 400 MMCs arrived in January 2024. Numbered 738 to 740 these buses were used on Flightline service 703. Like 731-737, these double-deckers also carried personalised registration marks FL73LHR, FL73WND and FL73LGO. These replaced 781 and 782 from this service. Although not intended for the Londonline service, generic grey liveried Enviro 400 City 741 (RG24BUS) became a common sight on the 702 service. By July 795 had lost Flightline livery.

## Arriva Southern Counties

Arriva Southern Counties Kent Thameside operation took over the Ware and Harlow garages of Arriva the Shires in 2016. The company operated route 310 between Hertford and Waltham Cross, just entering the TfL area. Fourteen Enviro 400 MMCs entered the fleet in the summer of 2016, replacing a fleet of Wright Eclipse Urban

**Arriva Kent** Thameside's 6491 (YY16YLB) is photographed unloading at Waltham Cross bus station having completed its journey from Hertford.

bodied Volvo B7RLEs. Numbered 6485 to 6498 these double-deckers were registered YY16YKU-X/Z, YLA-H/J. These were all allocated to Ware. 6485-90/2-5 were delivered in July, with 6491/6-8 following in August.

## Westway

Westway was the first of a handful of West London based independent operators to take stock of the Enviro 400 MMC double-decker. The first arrived in January 2017 carrying registration mark YY66PXR. It was joined in March by a second one registered YX17NUJ. These took up private registration marks 600SCX and 600CXS. Two more arrived in the summer of 2021, these being registered SK21FHV and SK21FHW respectively. These four double-deckers can be found operating various contracts in West London, as well as seeing service on rail replacement work.

## Uno

September 2017 saw a relaunch of the Hatfield to Queensbury via Edgware service operated by University Bus Limited, trading as Uno. For this route, six AD Enviro 400 City double-deckers were taken into stock wearing a pink and purple livery. The route was relaunched at this time as Comet, and appropriate branding was applied to the buses. Rolling stock numbers 250 to 255 were allocated to these buses which were registered YX17NPZ, NPY, NRE/F/J/K. Uno also used other AD Enviro 400 MMCs on the route as required.

## Imperial Coaches/NPC

Imperial Coaches was the second London independent to gain a fleet of Enviro 400 MMCs. The first quartet arrived in September 2017, these being registered YX67UYG/H/J/K. Almost two years passed before the next Enviro 400 MMCs were taken into stock, these carrying registration marks SK19EVP and SK19EVR. January 2020 saw the arrival of SL69XWU and SL69XWV; with SK70BVS/V being taken into stock in October 2020. The final pair materialised in April 2021 registered SK21FKA and SK21FKB.

New Punjab Coaches also operated a pair of Enviro 400 MMCs. SN18KSO was the first to arrive in June 2018. The second was taken into stock during December 2019. This slotted in with Imperial's January 2020 deliveries, registered SL69XWW.

## Westbus

Westbus is owned by the same company as Metroline (Comfort-Delgro). Between 2020 and 2023 three Enviro 400 MMCs were acquired by Westbus. The first two arrived in September 2020 wearing a red-based livery with a gold roof area. These were registered SK70BUH and SK70BUJ, with fleet numbers 191 and 192 being allotted to the pair. The third example was delivered to the company in May 2023 registered SK23CUJ. This was numbered 197 by the company.

**Westway's 600SCX** was originally registered YY66PXR. It is seen on rail replacement work at Luton Interchange.

**Uno's 251** (YX17NPY) is seen passing Edgware Station on its way to Queensbury. The 614 was relaunched in 2017 as the Comet, this branding, along with the key locations served, can be seen applied to the bus.

**Other Enviro** 400 MMCs owned by Uno are sometimes used on the 614. This is demonstrated by 256 (YX67VFW), which is also seen passing the entrance to Edgware Station.

**The photograph** below is another taken at Luton Interchange during a large rail replacement operation. Imperial Coaches SK19EVR is seen passing sister SK19EVP.

**London Travel** In took stock of two Enviro 400 MMCs in 2018. The second of the pair was SN18KLP which is captured by the camera rounding Marble Arch.

**Westbus took** stock of two AD Enviro 400 MMCs in September 2020. One of these was registered SK70BUJ, which is also seen at Luton Interchange whilst operating a rail replacement service for Thameslink.

## Other London-based operators

This small section looks at a few London-based independent operators that have also operated the Enviro 400 MMC. London Travel In purchased two in July 2018. These took up registration marks SN18KLO and SN18KLP.

Air Sym of Heathrow took an Enviro 400 MMC into stock in March 2021. This bus followed on from the two that were purchased by Westway in July 2021, taking up registration mark SK21FHX.

Erith-based Abbey Travel brought a solitary Enviro 400 MMC. This was registered SK71CKN and arrived in to stock during September 2021.

BM Coaches of Hayes purchased a pair of Enviro 400 MMCs in September 2022. These were registered SK72CWC and SK72CWD. They are used on various contracts as required by the company.

## First Berkshire

First Berkshire decided to upgrade two routes, the 7 (Britwell, Slough and Heathrow Terminal 5) and A4 (Heathrow Central Bus Station–Cippenham, Moreton Way) in 2023. Thirteen Enviro 400 MMC double-deckers were acquired from First Glasgow in early 2023. These carried rolling stock numbers 34375 to 34387 (SO68HFV/W/X/Y/Z, HGA/C/D/E/F and SK19EMF/J/V). 34375/6/8/81/3-6 arrived in February, with 34377/9/80/2/7 following in March. These 10.5m long Enviro 400 MMCs and were repainted into a orange livery with a purple rear before entering service. Their arrival saw the withdrawal of a fleet of Wright Eclipse Urban bodied Volvo B7RLEs and Volvo 9700 saloons that had previously operated the route.

## Carousel Buses

Carousel Buses of High Wycombe received a fleet of Enviro 400 MMCs from sister company Oxford Bus Company during the summer of 2024. Numbered 608 to 614 (RW/PS/PK/LM/GA/JG/GH64OXF) they were used by the company on route 102 between High Wycombe and Heathrow Airport. 608 arrived in May. The service operated under the Flightline brand, with a green-based livery being applied to them. 609 was the first to be treated, gaining the livery in April.

***Opposite above*: Thirteen Enviro 400 MMCs** were transferred from First Glasgow to First Berkshire in 2023. They were repainted into an orange and purple livery and used on two services in to Heathrow Airport. 34380 (SO68HGA) is seen paused in Slough town centre on its way to Heathrow Terminal 5 wearing this smart livery.

***Opposite below*: The network** of express services from the home counties to Heathrow Airport grew during 2023 and 2024. One new route introduced in 2024 was the Flightline 102 service linking High Wycombe with Heathrow. Six Enviro 400 MMCs passed from the Oxford Bus Company to fellow Go-Ahead group operator Carousel Buses. This included 609 (PS64OXF) which is seen departing High Wycombe bus station wearing the smart Flightline livery.

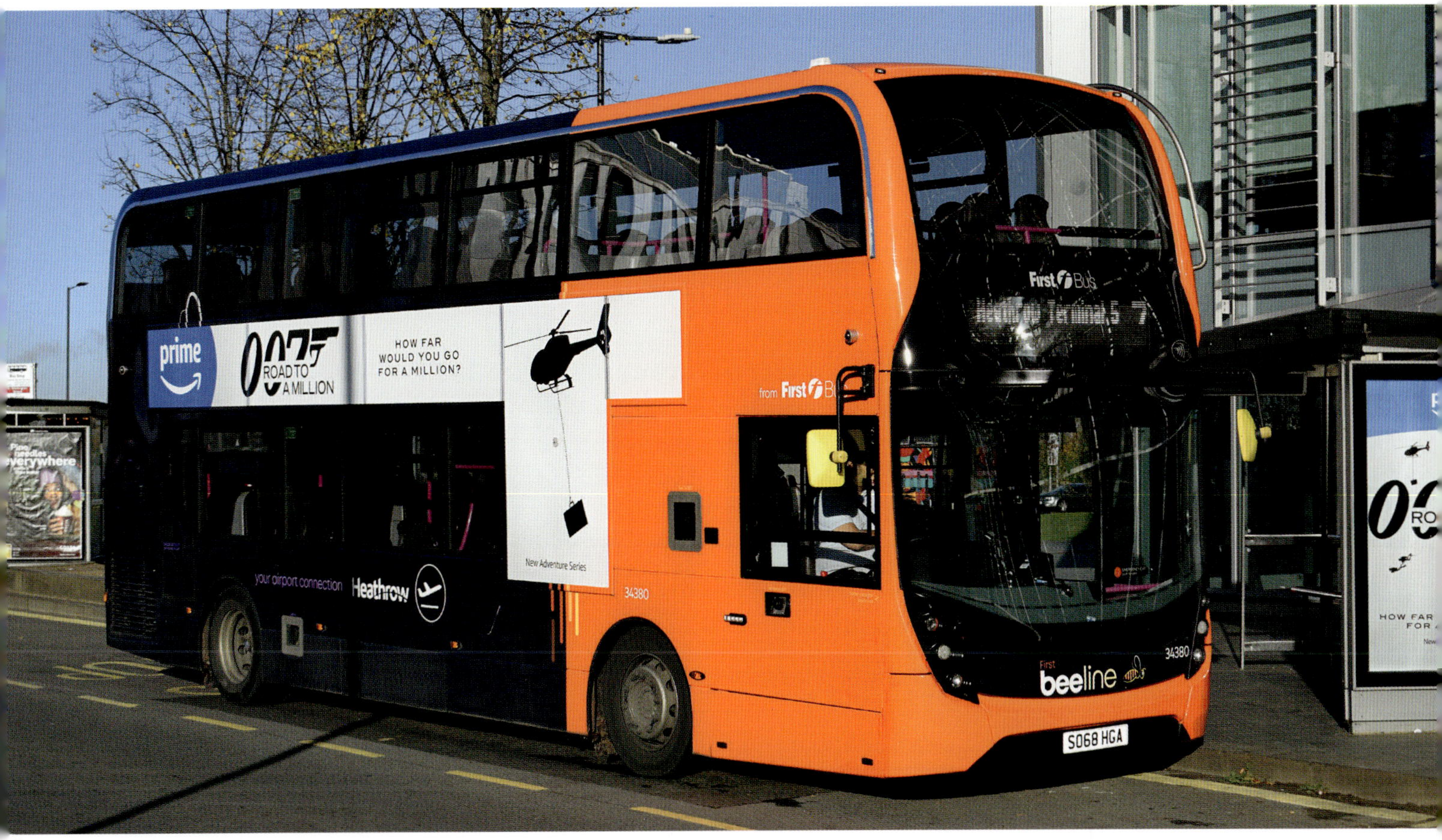
prime
007
ROAD TO
A MILLION
HOW FAR
WOULD YOU GO
FOR A MILLION?
New Adventure Series
your airport connection
Heathrow
34380
beeline
SO68 HGA

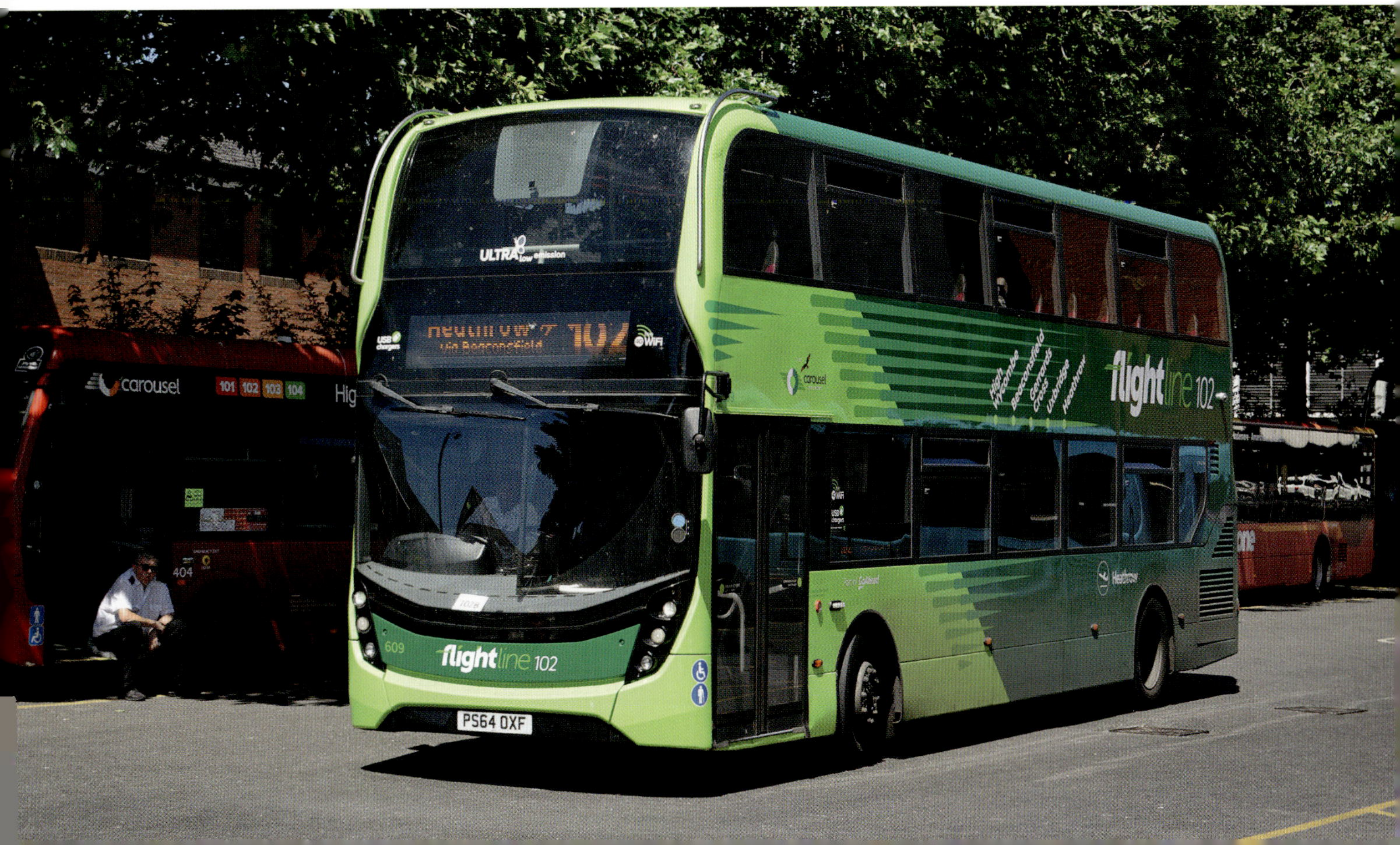
ULTRA low emission
carousel
101 102 103 104
flightline 102
609
PS64 DXF

# APPENDIX I: FLEET LISTS

This section of the book provides details of fleet numbers and registration marks. Unlike the main part of the book, the operators are listed in alphabetical order rather than in chronological order of when the Enviro 400 MMC/City' were received. Under each operator, the buses are also listed in numerical order.

## Demonstrator

| | YY64GXG | AD E40D | AD Enviro 400 MMC |
|---|---|---|---|

YY64GXG was new to Alexander Dennis Limited as a demonstrator. It was initially loaned to Abellio London before being acquired by the company.

## Abellio London

**2001 – 2053** **AD E40D Smart Hybrid** **AD Enviro 400 MMC**

| | | | | | | | | |
|---|---|---|---|---|---|---|---|---|
| 2001 | YX19ORG | Mar-19 | 2019 | YX20OCB | Mar-20 | 2037 | SK20BDZ | Jul-20 |
| 2002 | YX19ORH | Mar-19 | 2020 | YX20OCC | Mar-20 | 2038 | SK20BEJ | Jul-20 |
| 2003 | YX19ORJ | Mar-19 | 2021 | YX20OCD | Mar-20 | 2039 | SK20BEO | Jul-20 |
| 2004 | YX19ORK | Mar-19 | 2022 | SK20AZL | May-20 | 2040 | SK20BEU | Jul-20 |
| 2005 | YX19ORL | Mar-19 | 2023 | SK20AZN | May-20 | 2041 | SK20BEY | Jul-20 |
| 2006 | SN69ZRL | Dec-19 | 2024 | SK20AZO | May-20 | 2042 | SK20BFA | Jul-20 |
| 2007 | SN69ZRO | Dec-19 | 2025 | SK20AZP | May-20 | 2043 | SK20BFE | Jul-20 |
| 2008 | SN69ZRP | Dec-19 | 2026 | SK20AZR | May-20 | 2044 | SK20BFF | Jul-20 |
| 2009 | SN69ZRR | Dec-19 | 2027 | SK20AZT | May-20 | 2045 | SK20BFJ | Jul-20 |
| 2010 | SN69ZRT | Dec-19 | 2028 | SK20AZU | May-20 | 2046 | SK20BFL | Jul-20 |
| 2011 | SN69ZRU | Dec-19 | 2029 | SK20AZV | May-20 | 2047 | SK20BFM | Aug-20 |
| 2012 | SN69ZRV | Dec-19 | 2030 | SK20AZW | May-20 | 2048 | SK20BFN | Aug-20 |
| 2013 | YX20OBU | Mar-20 | 2031 | SK20AZX | May-20 | 2049 | SK20BFO | Aug-20 |
| 2014 | YX20OBV | Mar-20 | 2032 | SK20AZZ | May-20 | 2050 | SK20BFP | Aug-20 |
| 2015 | YX20OBW | Mar-20 | 2033 | SK20BAA | May-20 | 2051 | SK20BFU | Aug-20 |
| 2016 | YX20OBY | Mar-20 | 2034 | SK20BAO | May-20 | 2052 | SK20BFV | Aug-20 |
| 2017 | YX20OBZ | Mar-20 | 2035 | SK20BAU | May-20 | 2053 | SK20BFX | Aug-20 |
| 2018 | YX20OCA | Mar-20 | 2036 | SK20BAV | May-20 | | | |

**2487 – 2618** **AD E40H** **AD Enviro 400 MMC**

| | | | | | | | | |
|---|---|---|---|---|---|---|---|---|
| 2487 | YY64TYD | Dec-14 | 2531 | YX15OXA | Mar-15 | 2575 | YX17NVY | Apr-17 |
| 2488 | YY64TYF | Dec-14 | 2532 | YX15OXB | Jul-15 | 2576 | YX17NVZ | Apr-17 |
| 2489 | YY64TYG | Dec-14 | 2533 | YX15OXC | Jul-15 | 2577 | YX17NPP | Jul-17 |
| 2490 | YY64TYH | Dec-14 | 2534 | YY16YKA | Aug-16 | 2578 | YX17NPU | Jul-17 |
| 2491 | YY64TYK | Dec-14 | 2535 | YY16YKB | Aug-16 | 2579 | YX17NPV | Jul-17 |
| 2492 | YY64TYO | Dec-14 | 2536 | YY16YKC | Aug-16 | 2580 | YY67GZA | Oct-17 |
| 2493 | YY64TYP | Dec-14 | 2537 | YY16YKD | Aug-16 | 2581 | YY67GZB | Oct-17 |
| 2494 | YY64TYS | Dec-14 | 2538 | YY16YKE | Aug-16 | 2582 | YY67GZC | Oct-17 |
| 2495 | YY64TYT | Dec-14 | 2539 | YY16YKF | Aug-16 | 2583 | YY67GZD | Oct-17 |
| 2496 | YY64TYU | Dec-14 | 2540 | YY16YKG | Aug-16 | 2584 | YY67GZE | Oct-17 |
| 2497 | YY64TYV | Dec-14 | 2541 | YY16YKH | Aug-16 | 2585 | YY67GZF | Oct-17 |
| 2498 | YY64TYW | Dec-14 | 2542 | YY16YKJ | Aug-16 | 2586 | YY67GZG | Oct-17 |
| 2499 | YY64TYX | Jan-15 | 2543 | YY16YKK | Aug-16 | 2587 | YY67GZH | Oct-17 |
| 2500 | YY64TYZ | Jan-15 | 2544 | YY16YKL | Aug-16 | 2588 | YY67GZJ | Oct-17 |
| 2501 | YY64TZA | Jan-15 | 2545 | YY16YKM | Aug-16 | 2589 | YY67GZK | Oct-17 |
| 2502 | YY64TZB | Jan-15 | 2546 | YY16YKN | Aug-16 | 2590 | YY67GZL | Oct-17 |
| 2503 | YY64TZC | Jan-15 | 2547 | YY16YKO | Aug-16 | 2591 | YY67GZM | Oct-17 |
| 2504 | YY64TZD | Jan-15 | 2548 | YY16YKP | Aug-16 | 2592 | YY67GZN | Oct-17 |
| 2505 | YY64TZE | Jan-15 | 2549 | YY16YKR | Aug-16 | 2593 | YY67GZO | Oct-17 |
| 2506 | YY64TZF | Jan-15 | 2550 | YY16YKS | Aug-16 | 2594 | YY67GZP | Oct-17 |
| 2507 | YY64TZG | Jan-15 | 2551 | YY16YKT | Aug-16 | 2595 | YY67GZR | Oct-17 |
| 2508 | YY64TZH | Jan-15 | 2552 | YX17NUW | Mar-17 | 2596 | YY67GZS | Oct-17 |
| 2509 | YY64TZJ | Jan-15 | 2553 | YX17NUY | Mar-17 | 2597 | YY67GZT | Oct-17 |
| 2510 | YY64TZK | Jan-15 | 2554 | YX17NVA | Mar-17 | 2598 | YY67GZU | Oct-17 |
| 2511 | YY64TZL | Jan-15 | 2555 | YX17NVB | Mar-17 | 2599 | YY67GZV | Oct-17 |
| 2512 | YY64TZM | Jan-15 | 2556 | YX17NVC | Mar-17 | 2600 | YY67GZW | Oct-17 |
| 2513 | YY64TZN | Jan-15 | 2557 | YX17NVD | Mar-17 | 2601 | YY67GZX | Oct-17 |
| 2514 | YY64TZO | Jan-15 | 2558 | YX17NVE | Mar-17 | 2602 | YY67GZZ | Oct-17 |
| 2515 | YX15OWD | Mar-15 | 2559 | YX17NVF | Mar-17 | 2603 | SN18KKR | Apr-18 |
| 2516 | YX15OWE | Mar-15 | 2560 | YX17NVG | Mar-17 | 2604 | SN18KKS | Apr-18 |
| 2517 | YX15OWF | Mar-15 | 2561 | YX17NVH | Mar-17 | 2605 | SN18KKU | Apr-18 |
| 2518 | YX15OWG | Mar-15 | 2562 | YX17NVJ | Mar-17 | 2606 | SN18KKV | Apr-18 |
| 2519 | YX15OWH | Mar-15 | 2563 | YX17NVK | Mar-17 | 2607 | SN18KKW | Apr-18 |
| 2520 | YX15OWJ | Mar-15 | 2564 | YX17NVL | Mar-17 | 2608 | SN18KKX | Apr-18 |
| 2521 | YX15OWK | Mar-15 | 2565 | YX17NVM | Apr-17 | 2609 | SN18KKY | Apr-18 |
| 2522 | YX15OWM | Mar-15 | 2566 | YX17NVN | Apr-17 | 2610 | SN18KKZ | Apr-18 |
| 2523 | YX15OWO | Mar-15 | 2567 | YX17NVO | Apr-17 | 2611 | SN18KLA | Apr-18 |
| 2524 | YX15OWP | Mar-15 | 2568 | YX17NVP | Apr-17 | 2612 | SN18KLC | Apr-18 |
| 2525 | YX15OWR | Mar-15 | 2569 | YX17NVR | Apr-17 | 2613 | SN18KLD | Apr-18 |
| 2526 | YX15OWU | Mar-15 | 2570 | YX17NVS | Apr-17 | 2614 | SN18KLE | Apr-18 |
| 2527 | YX15OWV | Mar-15 | 2571 | YX17NVT | Apr-17 | 2615 | SN18KLF | Apr-18 |
| 2528 | YX15OWW | Mar-15 | 2572 | YX17NVU | Apr-17 | 2616 | SN18KLJ | Apr-18 |
| 2529 | YX15OWY | Mar-15 | 2573 | YX17NVV | Apr-17 | 2617 | SN18KLK | Apr-18 |
| 2530 | YX15OWZ | Mar-15 | 2574 | YX17NVW | Apr-17 | 2618 | SN18KLL | Apr-18 |

**3401 – 3441** **BYD D8UR DD** **AD Enviro 400 EV City**

| | | | | | | | | |
|---|---|---|---|---|---|---|---|---|
| 3401 | LC71KWJ | Nov-21 | 3415 | LC71KWY | Dec-21 | 3429 | LC71KXO | Feb-22 |
| 3402 | LC71KWK | Nov-21 | 3416 | LC71KWZ | Dec-21 | 3430 | LG22APK | May-22 |
| 3403 | LC71KWL | Dec-21 | 3417 | LC71KXA | Dec-21 | 3431 | LG22APO | May-22 |
| 3404 | LC71KWM | Nov-21 | 3418 | LC71KXB | Dec-21 | 3432 | LG22APU | May-22 |
| 3405 | LC71KWN | Nov-21 | 3419 | LC71KXD | Dec-21 | 3433 | LG22APV | May-22 |
| 3406 | LC71KWO | Dec-21 | 3420 | LC71KXE | Dec-21 | 3434 | LG22APX | May-22 |
| 3407 | LC71KWP | Nov-21 | 3421 | LC71KXF | Dec-21 | 3435 | LG22APY | May-22 |
| 3408 | LC71KWR | Nov-21 | 3422 | LC71KXG | Dec-21 | 3436 | LG22APZ | May-22 |
| 3409 | LC71KWS | Nov-21 | 3423 | LC71KXH | Dec-21 | 3437 | LG22ARF | May-22 |
| 3410 | LC71KWT | Dec-21 | 3424 | LC71KXJ | Dec-21 | 3438 | LG22ARO | May-22 |
| 3411 | LC71KWU | Dec-21 | 3425 | LC71KXK | Feb-22 | 3439 | LG22ARU | May-22 |
| 3412 | LC71KWV | Dec-21 | 3426 | LC71KXL | Feb-22 | 3440 | LG22ARX | May-22 |
| 3413 | LC71KWW | Dec-21 | 3427 | LC71KXM | Feb-22 | 3441 | LG22ARZ | May-22 |
| 3414 | LC71KWX | Dec-21 | 3428 | LC71KXN | Feb-22 | | | |

## Arriva London

**EA1 – EA22** **BYD D8UR DD** **AD Enviro 400 EV City**

| | | | | | | | | |
|---|---|---|---|---|---|---|---|---|
| EA 1 | LG71DJK | Aug-21 | EA 9 | LG71DKA | Sep-21 | EA17 | LG71DKU | Oct-21 |
| EA 2 | LG71DJO | Aug-21 | EA10 | LG71DKD | Sep-21 | EA18 | LG71DKV | Oct-21 |
| EA 3 | LG71DJU | Aug-21 | EA11 | LG71DKE | Sep-21 | EA19 | LG71DKX | Oct-21 |
| EA 4 | LG71DJV | Sep-21 | EA12 | LG71DKF | Sep-21 | EA20 | LG71DKY | Oct-21 |
| EA 5 | LG71DJX | Sep-21 | EA13 | LG71DKJ | Sep-21 | EA21 | LG71DLD | Oct-21 |
| EA 6 | LG71DJX | Sep-21 | EA14 | LG71DKL | Oct-21 | EA22 | LG71DLE | Nov-21 |
| EA 7 | LG71DJY | Sep-21 | EA15 | LG71DKN | Oct-21 | | | |
| EA 8 | LG71DJZ | Sep-21 | EA16 | LG71DKO | Oct-21 | | | |

**HA1 – HA53** **AD E40H** **AD Enviro 400 City**

| | | | | | | | | |
|---|---|---|---|---|---|---|---|---|
| HA 1 | LK65BYX | Nov-15 | HA11 | LK65BYM | Dec-15 | HA21 | LK66GZN | Nov-16 |
| HA 2 | LK65BYY | Nov-15 | HA12 | LK65BYN | Dec-15 | HA22 | LK66GZO | Nov-16 |
| HA 3 | LK65BYZ | Nov-15 | HA13 | LK65BYO | Dec-15 | HA23 | LK66GZP | Nov-16 |
| HA 4 | LK65BZA | Nov-15 | HA14 | LK65BYP | Dec-15 | HA24 | LK66GZS | Nov-16 |
| HA 5 | LK65BZB | Nov-15 | HA15 | LK65BYR | Dec-15 | HA25 | LK66GZT | Nov-16 |
| HA 6 | LK65BZC | Nov-15 | HA16 | LK65BYS | Jan-16 | HA26 | LK66GZU | Nov-16 |
| HA 7 | LK65BZD | Nov-15 | HA17 | LK65BYT | Dec-15 | HA27 | LK66GZV | Nov-16 |
| HA 8 | LK65BZE | Dec-15 | HA18 | LK65BYU | Dec-15 | HA28 | LK66GZW | Nov-16 |
| HA 9 | LK65BZF | Dec-15 | HA19 | LK65BYV | Jan-16 | HA29 | LK66GZY | Nov-16 |
| HA10 | LK65BZG | Dec-15 | HA20 | LK66GZM | Nov-16 | HA30 | LK66HAE | Dec-16 |

| | | | | | | | | |
|---|---|---|---|---|---|---|---|---|
| HA31 | LK66HAO | Dec-16 | HA39 | LK66HBG | Dec-16 | HA47 | LK66HBX | Dec-16 |
| HA32 | LK66HAX | Dec-16 | HA40 | LK66HBH | Dec-16 | HA48 | LK66HBY | Dec-16 |
| HA33 | LK66HBA | Dec-16 | HA41 | LK66HBJ | Dec-16 | HA49 | LK66HBZ | Dec-16 |
| HA34 | LK66HBB | Dec-16 | HA42 | LK66HBL | Dec-16 | HA50 | LK66HCA | Dec-16 |
| HA35 | LK66HBC | Dec-16 | HA43 | LK66HBN | Dec-16 | HA51 | LK66HCC | Dec-16 |
| HA36 | LK66HBD | Dec-16 | HA44 | LK66HBO | Dec-16 | HA52 | LK66HCD | Dec-16 |
| HA37 | LK66HBE | Dec-16 | HA45 | LK66HBP | Dec-16 | HA53 | LK66HCE | Dec-16 |
| HA38 | LK66HBF | Dec-16 | HA46 | LK66HBU | Dec-16 | | | |

**HT1 – HT28** **AD E40D Smart Hybrid** **AD Enviro 400 MMC**

| | | | | | | | | |
|---|---|---|---|---|---|---|---|---|
| HT 1 | SK20BFY | Aug-20 | HT11 | SK20BHA | Aug-20 | HT21 | SK70BVJ | Sep-20 |
| HT 2 | SK20BFZ | Aug-20 | HT12 | SK70BUU | Sep-20 | HT22 | SK70BVO | Sep-20 |
| HT 3 | SK20BGE | Aug-20 | HT13 | SK70BUV | Sep-20 | HT23 | SK70BVL | Sep-20 |
| HT 4 | SK20BGF | Aug-20 | HT14 | SK70BVE | Sep-20 | HT24 | SK70BVD | Sep-20 |
| HT 5 | SK20BGO | Aug-20 | HT15 | SK70BUW | Sep-20 | HT25 | SK70BVP | Sep-20 |
| HT 6 | SK20BGU | Aug-20 | HT16 | SK70BVF | Sep-20 | HT26 | SK70BVG | Sep-20 |
| HT 7 | SK20BGV | Aug-20 | HT17 | SK70BVA | Sep-20 | HT27 | SK70BVH | Sep-20 |
| HT 8 | SK20BGX | Aug-20 | HT18 | SK70BVN | Sep-20 | HT28 | SK70BVM | Oct-20 |
| HT 9 | SK20BGY | Aug-20 | HT19 | SK70BVB | Sep-20 | | | |
| HT10 | SK20BGZ | Aug-20 | HT20 | SK70BVC | Sep-20 | | | |

## CT Plus

**2501 – 2549** **AD E40H** **AD Enviro 400 City**

| | | | | | | | | |
|---|---|---|---|---|---|---|---|---|
| 2501 | SN16OHP | Jun-16 | 2518 | SN16OJH | Jun-16 | 2535 | SN66WRZ | Feb-17 |
| 2502 | SN16OHR | Jun-16 | 2519 | SN16OJJ | Jun-16 | 2536 | SN66WSD | Feb-17 |
| 2503 | SN16OHS | Jun-16 | 2520 | SN16OJK | Jun-16 | 2537 | SN66WSE | Feb-17 |
| 2504 | SN16OHT | Jun-16 | 2521 | SN16OJL | Jun-16 | 2538 | SN65OHP | Nov-15 |
| 2505 | SN16OHU | Jun-16 | 2522 | SN66WRE | Feb-17 | 2539 | YX19ORO | Mar-19 |
| 2506 | SN16OHV | Jun-16 | 2523 | SN66WRG | Feb-17 | 2540 | YX19ORP | Mar-19 |
| 2507 | SN16OHW | Jun-16 | 2524 | SN66WRJ | Feb-17 | 2541 | YX19ORS | Mar-19 |
| 2508 | SN16OHX | Jun-16 | 2525 | SN66WRK | Feb-17 | 2542 | YX19ORT | Mar-19 |
| 2509 | SN16OHY | Jun-16 | 2526 | SN66WRL | Feb-17 | 2543 | YX19ORU | Mar-19 |
| 2510 | SN16OHZ | Jun-16 | 2527 | SN66WRO | Feb-17 | 2544 | YX19ORV | Mar-19 |
| 2511 | SN16OJA | Jun-16 | 2528 | SN66WRP | Feb-17 | 2545 | YX19ORW | Mar-19 |
| 2512 | SN16OJB | Jun-16 | 2529 | SN66WRR | Feb-17 | 2546 | YX19ORY | Mar-19 |
| 2513 | SN16OJC | Jun-16 | 2530 | SN66WRT | Feb-17 | 2547 | YX19ORZ | Mar-19 |
| 2514 | SN16OJD | Jun-16 | 2531 | SN66WRU | Feb-17 | 2548 | YX69NLY | Oct-19 |
| 2515 | SN16OJE | Jun-16 | 2532 | SN66WRV | Feb-17 | 2549 | YX69NLZ | Oct-19 |
| 2516 | SN16OJF | Jun-16 | 2533 | SN66WRW | Feb-17 | | | |
| 2517 | SN16OJG | Jun-16 | 2534 | SN66WRX | Feb-17 | | | |

**2550 – 2551** **BYD D8UR DD** **AD Enviro 400 City EV**

| | | | | | |
|---|---|---|---|---|---|
| 2550e | LG21HZM | Mar-21 | 2551e | LG21HZN | Mar-21 |

# Go-Ahead London

| | | | | |
|---|---|---|---|---|
| E284 | SN66WNE | AD E40D | AD Enviro 400 MMC | Feb-17 |
| E285 | SN66WNF | AD E40D | AD Enviro 400 MMC | Feb-17 |

**Ee1-Ee49** **BYD D8UR DD** **AD Enviro 400EV City**

| | | | | | | | | |
|---|---|---|---|---|---|---|---|---|
| Ee 1 | LF20XLA | Mar-20 | Ee 18 | LF20XLU | Mar-20 | Ee 35 | LF20XMO | Apr-20 |
| Ee 2 | LF20XLB | Mar-20 | Ee 19 | LF20XLV | Mar-20 | Ee 36 | LF20XMP | Apr-20 |
| Ee 3 | LF20XLC | Mar-20 | Ee 20 | LF20XLW | Mar-20 | Ee 37 | LF20XMR | Apr-20 |
| Ee 4 | LF20XLD | Mar-20 | Ee 21 | LF20XLX | Mar-20 | Ee 38 | LF20XNG | May-20 |
| Ee 5 | LF20XLE | Mar-20 | Ee 22 | LF20XLY | Mar-20 | Ee 39 | LF20XNJ | May-20 |
| Ee 6 | LF20XLG | Mar-20 | Ee 23 | LF20XLZ | Mar-20 | Ee 40 | LF20XNK | May-20 |
| Ee 7 | LF20XLH | Mar-20 | Ee 24 | LF20XMA | Mar-20 | Ee 41 | LF20XNL | May-20 |
| Ee 8 | LF20XLJ | Mar-20 | Ee 25 | LF20XMB | Mar-20 | Ee 42 | LF20XNM | May-20 |
| Ee 9 | LF20XLK | Mar-20 | Ee 26 | LF20XMC | Mar-20 | Ee 43 | LF20XNN | May-20 |
| Ee 10 | LF20XLL | Mar-20 | Ee 27 | LF20XMD | Mar-20 | Ee 44 | LF20XNO | May-20 |
| Ee 11 | LF20XLM | Mar-20 | Ee 28 | LF20XME | Mar-20 | Ee 45 | LF20XNP | May-20 |
| Ee 12 | LF20LXN | Mar-20 | Ee 29 | LF20XMG | Mar-20 | Ee 46 | LF20XNR | May-20 |
| Ee 13 | LF20XLO | Mar-20 | Ee 30 | LF20XMH | Mar-20 | Ee 47 | LF20XNS | May-20 |
| Ee 14 | LF20XLP | Mar-20 | Ee 31 | LF20XMJ | Apr-20 | Ee 48 | LF20XNT | May-20 |
| Ee 15 | LF20XLR | Mar-20 | Ee 32 | LF20XMK | Mar-20 | Ee 49 | LF20XNU | May-20 |
| Ee 16 | LF20XLS | Mar-20 | Ee 33 | LF20XML | Apr-20 | | | |
| Ee 17 | LF20XLT | Mar-20 | Ee 34 | LF20XMM | Apr-20 | | | |

**Ee50 – Ee69** **BYD D8UR DD** **AD Enviro 400EV City**

| | | | | | | | | |
|---|---|---|---|---|---|---|---|---|
| Ee 50 | LG21JFZ | Apr-21 | Ee 57 | LG21JHA | Apr-21 | Ee 64 | LG21JHO | Apr-21 |
| Ee 51 | LG21JGF | Apr-21 | Ee 58 | LG21JHE | Apr-21 | Ee 65 | LG21JHU | Apr-21 |
| Ee 52 | LG21JGO | Apr-21 | Ee 59 | LG21JHF | Apr-21 | Ee 66 | LG21JHV | Apr-21 |
| Ee 53 | LG21JGU | Apr-21 | Ee 60 | LG21JHH | Apr-21 | Ee 67 | LG21JHX | Apr-21 |
| Ee 54 | LG21JGV | Apr-21 | Ee 61 | LG21JHJ | Apr-21 | Ee 68 | LG21JHZ | Apr-21 |
| Ee 55 | LG21JGX | Apr-21 | Ee 62 | LG21JHK | Apr-21 | Ee 69 | LG21JJE | Apr-21 |
| Ee 56 | LG212JGZ | Apr-21 | Ee 63 | LG21JHL | Apr-21 | | | |

**Ee70 – Ee93** **BYD D8UR DD** **AD Enviro 400EV City**

| | | | | | | | | |
|---|---|---|---|---|---|---|---|---|
| Ee 70 | LG72DNO | Oct-22 | Ee 74 | LG72DNY | Oct-22 | Ee 78 | LG72DOU | Oct-22 |
| Ee 71 | LG72DNU | Oct-22 | Ee 75 | LG72DOA | Oct-22 | Ee 79 | LG72DPE | Oct-22 |
| Ee 72 | LG72DNV | Oct-22 | Ee 76 | LG72DOH | Oct-22 | Ee 80 | LG72DPF | Oct-22 |
| Ee 73 | LG72DNX | Oct-22 | Ee 77 | LG72DOJ | Oct-22 | Ee 81 | LG72DPK | Oct-22 |

| | | | | | | | | |
|---|---|---|---|---|---|---|---|---|
| Ee 82 | LG72DPN | Oct-22 | Ee 86 | LG72DPX | Oct-22 | Ee 90 | LG72DRV | Oct-22 |
| Ee 83 | LG72DPO | Oct-22 | Ee 87 | LG72DPY | Oct-22 | Ee 91 | LG72DRX | Oct-22 |
| Ee 84 | LG72DPU | Oct-22 | Ee 88 | LG72DPZ | Oct-22 | Ee 92 | LG72DRZ | Oct-22 |
| Ee 85 | LG72DPV | Oct-22 | Ee 89 | LG72DRO | Oct-22 | Ee 93 | LG72DSE | Oct-22 |

**Ee94 – Ee93** **BYD D8UR DD** **AD Enviro 400EV City**

| | | | | | | | | |
|---|---|---|---|---|---|---|---|---|
| Ee 94 | LG23FJD | Jun-23 | Ee130 | LG23FAF | Mar-23 | Ee166 | LG23EZL | Mar-23 |
| Ee 95 | LG23FJE | Jun-23 | Ee131 | LG23FAJ | Mar-23 | Ee167 | LG23EZM | Mar-23 |
| Ee 96 | LG23FJF | Jun-23 | Ee132 | LG23FAK | Mar-23 | Ee168 | LG23EZN | Mar-23 |
| Ee 97 | LG23FJJ | Jun-23 | Ee133 | LG23FAM | Mar-23 | Ee169 | LG23EZO | Mar-23 |
| Ee 98 | LG23FJK | Jun-23 | Ee134 | LG23FAO | Mar-23 | Ee170 | LG23EZP | Mar-23 |
| Ee 99 | LG23FJN | Jun-23 | Ee135 | LG23FAU | Mar-23 | Ee171 | LG23EZR | Mar-23 |
| Ee100 | LG23FJO | Jun-23 | Ee136 | LG23FBA | Mar-23 | Ee172 | LG23EUN | Jul-23 |
| Ee101 | LD72XZT | Feb-23 | Ee137 | LG23FBB | Mar-23 | Ee173 | LG23EUO | Jul-23 |
| Ee102 | LD72XZU | Feb-23 | Ee138 | LG23FBC | Mar-23 | Ee174 | LG23EUP | Jul-23 |
| Ee103 | LD72XZV | Feb-23 | Ee139 | LG23FBD | Mar-23 | Ee175 | LG23EUR | Jul-23 |
| Ee104 | LD72XZW | Feb-23 | Ee140 | LG23FBE | Mar-23 | Ee176 | LG23EUT | Jul-23 |
| Ee105 | LD72XZX | Feb-23 | Ee141 | LG23FBF | Mar-23 | Ee177 | LG23EUU | Jul-23 |
| Ee106 | LD72XZY | Feb-23 | Ee142 | LG23FBJ | Mar-23 | Ee178 | LG23EUV | Jul-23 |
| Ee107 | LD72XZZ | Feb-23 | Ee143 | LG23FBK | Mar-23 | Ee179 | LG23EUW | Jul-23 |
| Ee108 | LD72YAA | Feb-23 | Ee144 | LG23FBL | Mar-23 | Ee180 | LG23EUX | Jul-23 |
| Ee109 | LD72YAE | Feb-23 | Ee145 | LD72UHT | Feb-23 | Ee181 | LG23EUY | Jul-23 |
| Ee110 | LD72YAF | Feb-23 | Ee146 | LD72UHU | Feb-23 | Ee182 | LG23EUZ | Jul-23 |
| Ee111 | LD72YAG | Feb-23 | Ee147 | LD72UHV | Feb-23 | Ee183 | LG23EVB | Jul-23 |
| Ee112 | LD72YAH | Mar-23 | Ee148 | LD72UHW | Mar-23 | Ee184 | LG23EVC | Jul-23 |
| Ee113 | LG23FFV | Feb-23 | Ee149 | LD72UHX | Mar-23 | Ee185 | LG23EVD | Jul-23 |
| Ee114 | LG23FFW | Feb-23 | Ee150 | LD72UHY | Mar-23 | Ee186 | LG23EVF | Jul-23 |
| Ee115 | LG23FFX | Feb-23 | Ee151 | LG23FGU | Mar-23 | Ee187 | LB23PFU | Sep-23 |
| Ee116 | LG23FFY | Feb-23 | Ee152 | LG23FGV | Mar-23 | Ee188 | LB23PFV | Sep-23 |
| Ee117 | LG23FFZ | Mar-23 | Ee153 | LG23FGX | Mar-23 | Ee189 | LB23PFX | Sep-23 |
| Ee118 | LG23FGA | Mar-23 | Ee154 | LG23FGZ | Mar-23 | Ee190 | LB23PFY | Sep-23 |
| Ee119 | LG23FGC | Mar-23 | Ee155 | LG23FHA | Mar-23 | Ee191 | LB23PFZ | Sep-23 |
| Ee120 | LG23FGD | Mar-23 | Ee156 | LG23FHB | Mar-23 | Ee192 | LB23PGE | Sep-23 |
| Ee121 | LG23FGE | Mar-23 | Ee157 | LG23FHC | Mar-23 | Ee193 | LB23PGF | Sep-23 |
| Ee122 | LG23FGF | Mar-23 | Ee158 | LG23FHD | Mar-23 | Ee194 | LB23PGK | Sep-23 |
| Ee123 | LG23FGJ | Mar-23 | Ee159 | LG23FHE | Mar-23 | Ee195 | LB23PGO | Sep-23 |
| Ee124 | LG23FGK | Mar-23 | Ee160 | LG23FHF | Mar-23 | Ee196 | LB23PGU | Sep-23 |
| Ee125 | LG23FGM | Mar-23 | Ee161 | LG23FHH | Mar-23 | Ee197 | LB23PGV | Sep-23 |
| Ee126 | LG23FGN | Mar-23 | Ee162 | LG23FHJ | Mar-23 | Ee198 | LB23PGX | Sep-23 |
| Ee127 | LG23FGO | Mar-23 | Ee163 | LG23EZH | Mar-23 | Ee199 | LB23PGY | Sep-23 |
| Ee128 | LG23FGP | Mar-23 | Ee164 | LG23EZJ | Mar-23 | Ee200 | LB23PGZ | Sep-23 |
| Ee129 | LG23FAA | Mar-23 | Ee165 | LG23EZK | Mar-23 | | | |

**Ee201 – Ee242** **BYD D8UR DD** **AD Enviro 400EV City**

| | | | | | | | | |
|---|---|---|---|---|---|---|---|---|
| Ee201 | LG73FTJ | Sep-23 | Ee215 | LF24ZKH | Mar-24 | Ee229 | LG73FRO | Oct-23 |
| Ee202 | LG73FTK | Sep-23 | Ee216 | LF24ZKJ | Mar-24 | Ee230 | LG73FRP | Oct-23 |
| Ee203 | LG73FTN | Sep-23 | Ee217 | LF24ZKK | Mar-24 | Ee231 | LG73FRR | Oct-23 |
| Ee204 | LG73FTO | Sep-23 | Ee218 | LG73FPV | Oct-23 | Ee232 | LG73FRU | Oct-23 |
| Ee205 | LF24ZJV | Mar-24 | Ee219 | LG73FPX | Oct-23 | Ee233 | LG73FRV | Oct-23 |
| Ee206 | LF24ZJX | Mar-24 | Ee220 | LG73FPY | Oct-23 | Ee234 | LG73FRX | Oct-23 |
| Ee207 | LF24ZJY | Mar-24 | Ee221 | LG73FPZ | Oct-23 | Ee235 | LG73FRZ | Oct-23 |
| Ee208 | LF24ZJZ | Mar-24 | Ee222 | LG73FRC | Oct-23 | Ee236 | LG73FSA | Oct-23 |
| Ee209 | LF24ZKA | Mar-24 | Ee223 | LG73FRD | Oct-23 | Ee237 | LG73FSC | Oct-23 |
| Ee210 | LF24ZKB | Mar-24 | Ee224 | LG73FRF | Oct-23 | Ee238 | LG73FSD | Oct-23 |
| Ee211 | LF24ZKC | Mar-24 | Ee225 | LG73FRJ | Oct-23 | Ee239 | LG73FSE | Oct-23 |
| Ee212 | LF24ZKD | Mar-24 | Ee226 | LG73FRK | Oct-23 | Ee240 | LG73FSF | Oct-23 |
| Ee213 | LF24ZKE | Mar-24 | Ee227 | LG73FRL | Oct-23 | Ee241 | LG73FSJ | Oct-23 |
| Ee214 | LF24ZKG | Mar-24 | Ee228 | LG73FRN | Oct-23 | Ee242 | LG73FSK | Oct-23 |

**Ee243 – Ee273** **BYD D8UR DD** **AD Enviro 400EV City**

| | | | | | | | | |
|---|---|---|---|---|---|---|---|---|
| Ee243 | LF24ZGC | Mar-24 | Ee254 | LF24ZGP | Mar-24 | Ee265 | LF24ZNY | Jun-24 |
| Ee244 | LF24ZGD | Mar-24 | Ee255 | LF24ZGR | Mar-24 | Ee266 | LF24ZNZ | Jun-24 |
| Ee245 | LF24ZGE | Mar-24 | Ee256 | LF24ZGS | Mar-24 | Ee267 | LF24ZPB | Jun-24 |
| Ee246 | LF24ZGG | Mar-24 | Ee257 | LF24ZGT | Mar-24 | Ee268 | LF24ZPC | Jun-24 |
| Ee247 | LF24ZGH | Mar-24 | Ee258 | LF24ZGU | Mar-24 | Ee269 | LF24ZPD | Jun-24 |
| Ee248 | LF24ZGJ | Mar-24 | Ee259 | LF24ZGV | Mar-24 | Ee270 | LF24ZPE | Jun-24 |
| Ee249 | LF24ZGK | Mar-24 | Ee260 | LF24ZGW | Mar-24 | Ee271 | LF24ZPG | Jun-24 |
| Ee250 | LF24ZGL | Mar-24 | Ee261 | LF24ZGX | Mar-24 | Ee272 | LF24ZPH | Jun-24 |
| Ee251 | LF24ZGM | Mar-24 | Ee262 | LF24ZGY | Mar-24 | Ee273 | LF24ZPJ | Jun-24 |
| Ee252 | LF24ZGN | Mar-24 | Ee263 | LF24ZNW | Jun-24 | | | |
| Ee253 | LF24ZGO | Mar-24 | Ee264 | LF24ZNX | Jun-24 | | | |

**EH39 – EH60** **AD E40H** **AD Enviro 400 MMC**

| | | | | | | | | |
|---|---|---|---|---|---|---|---|---|
| EH 39 | YX16OBT | Mar-16 | EH 47 | YX16OCC | Apr-16 | EH 55 | YX16OCM | Apr-16 |
| EH 40 | YX16OBU | Mar-16 | EH 48 | YX16OCD | Apr-16 | EH 56 | YX16OCN | Apr-16 |
| EH 41 | YX16OBV | Mar-16 | EH 49 | YX16OCE | Apr-16 | EH 57 | YX16OCO | Apr-16 |
| EH 42 | YX16OBW | Mar-16 | EH 50 | YX16OCF | Apr-16 | EH 58 | YX16OCP | Apr-16 |
| EH 43 | YX16OBY | Mar-16 | EH 51 | YX16OCG | Apr-16 | EH 59 | YX16OCR | Apr-16 |
| EH 44 | YX16OBZ | Mar-16 | EH 52 | YX16OCH | Apr-16 | EH 60 | YX16OCS | Apr-16 |
| EH 45 | YX16OCA | Mar-16 | EH 53 | YX16OCJ | Apr-16 | | | |
| EH 46 | YX16OCB | Mar-16 | EH 54 | YX16OCL | Apr-16 | | | |

**EH61 – EH112** **AD E40H** **AD Enviro 400 MMC**

| | | | | | | | | |
|---|---|---|---|---|---|---|---|---|
| EH 61 | YX66WHC | Oct-16 | EH 79 | YY66OYH | Dec-16 | EH 97 | YY66OZC | Jan-17 |
| EH 62 | YX66WHD | Oct-16 | EH 80 | YY66OYJ | Dec-16 | EH 98 | YY66OZD | Jan-17 |
| EH 63 | YX66WHE | Nov-16 | EH 81 | YY66OYK | Dec-16 | EH 99 | YY66OZE | Jan-17 |
| EH 64 | YX66WHF | Nov-16 | EH 82 | YY66OYL | Jan-17 | EH100 | YY66OZF | Jan-17 |
| EH 65 | YX66WHG | Oct-16 | EH 83 | YY66OYM | Jan-17 | EH101 | YY66OZG | Jan-17 |
| EH 66 | YX66WHH | Nov-16 | EH 84 | YY66OYN | Jan-17 | EH102 | YY66OZH | Jan-17 |
| EH 67 | YX66WHJ | Nov-16 | EH 85 | YY66OYO | Jan-17 | EH103 | YY66OZJ | Jan-17 |
| EH 68 | YX66WHK | Nov-16 | EH 86 | YY66OYP | Jan-17 | EH104 | YY66OZK | Jan-17 |
| EH 69 | YX66WHL | Nov-16 | EH 87 | YY66OYR | Jan-17 | EH105 | YY66OZL | Jan-17 |
| EH 70 | YX66WHM | Nov-16 | EH 88 | YY66OYS | Jan-17 | EH106 | YY66OZM | Jan-17 |
| EH 71 | YX66WHN | Nov-16 | EH 89 | YY66OYT | Jan-17 | EH107 | YY66OZO | Jan-17 |
| EH 72 | YX66WHP | Nov-16 | EH 90 | YY66OYU | Jan-17 | EH108 | YY66OZP | Jan-17 |
| EH 73 | YX66WHR | Nov-16 | EH 91 | YY66OYV | Jan-17 | EH109 | YY66OZR | Jan-17 |
| EH 74 | YY66OYB | Nov-16 | EH 92 | YY66OYW | Jan-17 | EH110 | YY66OZS | Jan-17 |
| EH 75 | YY66OYC | Dec-16 | EH 93 | YY66OYX | Jan-17 | EH111 | YY66OZT | Jan-17 |
| EH 76 | YY66OYE | Dec-16 | EH 94 | YY66OYZ | Jan-17 | EH112 | YY66OZU | Jan-17 |
| EH 77 | YY66OYF | Dec-16 | EH 95 | YY66OZA | Jan-17 | | | |
| EH 78 | YY66OYG | Dec-16 | EH 96 | YY66OZB | Jan-17 | | | |

**EH113 – EH130** **AD E40H** **AD Enviro 400 MMC**

| | | | | | | | | |
|---|---|---|---|---|---|---|---|---|
| EH113 | SN66WNY | Jan-17 | EH119 | SN66WOH | Jan-17 | EH125 | SN66WOX | Jan-17 |
| EH114 | SN66WNZ | Jan-17 | EH120 | SN66WOJ | Jan-17 | EH126 | SN66WOY | Jan-17 |
| EH115 | SN66WOA | Jan-17 | EH121 | SN66WOM | Jan-17 | EH127 | SN66WPA | Jan-17 |
| EH116 | SN66WOB | Jan-17 | EH122 | SN66WOR | Jan-17 | EH128 | SN66WPD | Jan-17 |
| EH117 | SN66WOC | Jan-17 | EH123 | SN66WOU | Jan-17 | EH129 | SN66WPE | Jan-17 |
| EH118 | SN66WOD | Jan-17 | EH124 | SN66WOV | Jan-17 | EH130 | SN66WPF | Jan-17 |

**EH131 – EH160** **AD E40H** **AD Enviro 400 MMC**

| | | | | | | | | |
|---|---|---|---|---|---|---|---|---|
| EH131 | YW17JTV | Aug-17 | EH142 | YW17JUO | Aug-17 | EH153 | YW17JVG | Aug-17 |
| EH132 | YW17JTX | Aug-17 | EH143 | YW17JUT | Aug-17 | EH154 | YW17JVH | Aug-17 |
| EH133 | YW17JTY | Aug-17 | EH144 | YW17JUU | Aug-17 | EH155 | YW17JVJ | Aug-17 |
| EH134 | YW17JTZ | Aug-17 | EH145 | YW17JUV | Aug-17 | EH156 | YW17JVK | Aug-17 |
| EH135 | YW17JUA | Aug-17 | EH146 | YW17JUX | Aug-17 | EH157 | YW17JVL | Aug-17 |
| EH136 | YW17JUC | Aug-17 | EH147 | YW17JUY | Aug-17 | EH158 | YW17JVM | Aug-17 |
| EH137 | YW17JUE | Aug-17 | EH148 | YW17JVA | Aug-17 | EH159 | YW17JVN | Aug-17 |
| EH138 | YW17JUF | Aug-17 | EH149 | YW17JVC | Aug-17 | EH160 | YW17JVO | Aug-17 |
| EH139 | YW17JUH | Aug-17 | EH150 | YW17JVD | Aug-17 | EH161 | YW17JVP | Aug-17 |
| EH140 | YW17JUJ | Aug-17 | EH151 | YW17JVE | Aug-17 | | | |
| EH141 | YW17JUK | Aug-17 | EH152 | YW17JVF | Aug-17 | | | |

**EH162 – EH170** **AD E40H** **AD Enviro 400 MMC**

| | | | | | | | | |
|---|---|---|---|---|---|---|---|---|
| EH162 | YX67VFG | Oct-17 | EH165 | YX67VFK | Oct-17 | EH168 | YX67VFN | Oct-17 |
| EH163 | YX67VFH | Oct-17 | EH166 | YX67VFL | Oct-17 | EH169 | YX67VFO | Oct-17 |
| EH164 | YX67VFJ | Oct-17 | EH167 | YX67VFM | Oct-17 | EH170 | YX67VFP | Oct-17 |

**EH171-EH224** **AD E40H** **AD Enviro 400 MMC**

| | | | | | | | | |
|---|---|---|---|---|---|---|---|---|
| EH171 | YY67UPX | Jan-18 | EH189 | YY67URT | Jan-18 | EH207 | YY67UTG | Feb-18 |
| EH172 | YY67UPZ | Jan-18 | EH190 | YY67URU | Jan-18 | EH208 | YY67UTH | Feb-18 |
| EH173 | YY67URA | Jan-18 | EH191 | YY67URV | Jan-18 | EH209 | YY67UTJ | Feb-18 |
| EH174 | YY67URB | Jan-18 | EH192 | YY67URW | Jan-18 | EH210 | YY67UTK | Feb-18 |
| EH175 | YY67URC | Jan-18 | EH193 | YY67URX | Jan-18 | EH211 | YY67UTL | Feb-18 |
| EH176 | YY67URE | Jan-18 | EH194 | YY67URZ | Jan-18 | EH212 | YY67UTM | Feb-18 |
| EH177 | YY67URF | Jan-18 | EH195 | YY67USS | Feb-18 | EH213 | YY67UTN | Feb-18 |
| EH178 | YY67URG | Jan-18 | EH196 | YY67UST | Feb-18 | EH214 | YY67UTO | Feb-18 |
| EH179 | YY67URH | Jan-18 | EH197 | YY67USU | Feb-18 | EH215 | YX18KPA | Mar-18 |
| EH180 | YY67URJ | Jan-18 | EH198 | YY67USV | Feb-18 | EH216 | YX18KPE | Mar-18 |
| EH181 | YY67URK | Jan-18 | EH199 | YY67USW | Feb-18 | EH217 | YX18KPF | Mar-18 |
| EH182 | YY67URL | Jan-18 | EH200 | YY67USX | Feb-18 | EH218 | YX18KPG | Mar-18 |
| EH183 | YY67URM | Jan-18 | EH201 | YY67USZ | Feb-18 | EH219 | YX18KPJ | Mar-18 |
| EH184 | YY67URN | Jan-18 | EH202 | YY67UTA | Feb-18 | EH220 | YX18KPK | Mar-18 |
| EH185 | YY67URO | Jan-18 | EH203 | YY67UTB | Feb-18 | EH221 | YX18KPL | Mar-18 |
| EH186 | YY67URP | Jan-18 | EH204 | YY67UTC | Feb-18 | EH222 | YX18KPN | Mar-18 |
| EH187 | YY67URR | Jan-18 | EH205 | YY67UTE | Feb-18 | EH223 | YX18KPO | Mar-18 |
| EH188 | YY67URS | Jan-18 | EH206 | YY67UTF | Feb-18 | EH224 | YX18KPP | Mar-18 |

**EH225 – EH263** **AD E40H** **AD Enviro 400 MMC**

| | | | | | | | | |
|---|---|---|---|---|---|---|---|---|
| EH225 | YX18KYY | Jun-18 | EH238 | YX18KRN | Apr-18 | EH251 | YX18KSY | Apr-18 |
| EH226 | YX18KPR | Apr-18 | EH239 | YX18KRO | Apr-18 | EH252 | YX18KSZ | Apr-18 |
| EH227 | YX18KPT | Apr-18 | EH240 | YX18KRU | Apr-18 | EH253 | YX18KTA | Apr-18 |
| EH228 | YX18KPU | Apr-18 | EH241 | YX18KRV | Apr-18 | EH254 | YX18KTC | Apr-18 |
| EH229 | YX18KPV | Apr-18 | EH242 | YX18KRZ | Apr-18 | EH255 | YX18KTD | Apr-18 |
| EH230 | YX18KPY | Apr-18 | EH243 | YX18KSE | Apr-18 | EH256 | YX18KTE | Apr-18 |
| EH231 | YX18KPZ | Apr-18 | EH244 | YX18KSF | Apr-18 | EH257 | YX18KTF | Apr-18 |
| EH232 | YX18KRD | Apr-18 | EH245 | YX18KSJ | Apr-18 | EH258 | YX18KTG | Apr-18 |
| EH233 | YX18KRE | Apr-18 | EH246 | YX18KSK | Apr-18 | EH259 | YX18KTJ | Apr-18 |
| EH234 | YX18KRF | Apr-18 | EH247 | YX18KSN | Apr-18 | EH260 | YX18KTK | Apr-18 |
| EH235 | YX18KRG | Apr-18 | EH248 | YX18KSO | Apr-18 | EH261 | YX18KTL | Apr-18 |
| EH236 | YX18KRJ | Apr-18 | EH249 | YX18KSU | Apr-18 | EH262 | YX18KTN | Apr-18 |
| EH237 | YX18KRK | Apr-18 | EH250 | YX18KSV | Apr-18 | EH263 | YX18KTO | Apr-18 |

Note: EH225-263 were examples of the AD E40H Ultra Cap

**EH264 – EH284** **AD E40H** **AD Enviro 400 MMC**

| | | | | | | | | |
|---|---|---|---|---|---|---|---|---|
| EH264 | SN18KLU | Apr-18 | EH271 | SN18KMG | Apr-18 | EH278 | SN18KMX | Apr-18 |
| EH265 | SN18KLV | Apr-18 | EH272 | SN18KMJ | Apr-18 | EH279 | SN18KMY | Apr-18 |
| EH266 | SN18KLX | Apr-18 | EH273 | SN18KMK | Apr-18 | EH280 | SN18KMZ | Apr-18 |
| EH267 | SN18KLZ | Apr-18 | EH274 | SN18KMM | Apr-18 | EH281 | SN18KNA | Apr-18 |
| EH268 | SN18KMA | Apr-18 | EH275 | SN18KMO | Apr-18 | EH282 | SN18KNB | Apr-18 |
| EH269 | SN18KME | Apr-18 | EH276 | SN18KMU | Apr-18 | EH283 | SN18KNC | Apr-18 |
| EH270 | SN18KMF | Apr-18 | EH277 | SN18KMV | Apr-18 | EH284 | SN18KND | Apr-18 |

**EH285 – EH310** **AD E40H** **AD Enviro 400 MMC**

| | | | | | | | | |
|---|---|---|---|---|---|---|---|---|
| EH285 | YX18KWW | Jun-18 | EH294 | YX18KXG | Jun-18 | EH303 | YX18KXR | Jun-18 |
| EH286 | YX18KWY | Jun-18 | EH295 | YX18KXH | Jun-18 | EH304 | YX18KXS | Jun-18 |
| EH287 | YX18KWZ | Jun-18 | EH296 | YX18KXJ | Jun-18 | EH305 | YX18KXT | Jun-18 |
| EH288 | YX18KXA | Jun-18 | EH297 | YX18KXK | Jun-18 | EH306 | YX18KXU | Jun-18 |
| EH289 | YX18KXB | Jun-18 | EH298 | YX18KXL | Jun-18 | EH307 | YX18KXV | Jun-18 |
| EH290 | YX18KXC | Jun-18 | EH299 | YX18KXM | Jun-18 | EH308 | YX18KXW | Jun-18 |
| EH291 | YX18KXD | Jun-18 | EH300 | YX18KXN | Jun-18 | EH309 | YX18KXY | Jun-18 |
| EH292 | YX18KXE | Jun-18 | EH301 | YX18KXO | Jun-18 | EH310 | YX18KXZ | Jun-18 |
| EH293 | YX18KXF | Jun-18 | EH302 | YX18KXP | Jun-18 | | | |

**EH311 – EH343** **AD E40H** **AD Enviro 400 MMC**

| | | | | | | | | |
|---|---|---|---|---|---|---|---|---|
| EH311 | YW19VPC | Jul-19 | EH322 | YW19VPP | Jul-19 | EH333 | YW19VVF | Aug-19 |
| EH312 | YW19VPD | Jul-19 | EH323 | YW19VPR | Jul-19 | EH334 | YW19VVG | Aug-19 |
| EH313 | YW19VPE | Jul-19 | EH324 | YW19VPT | Jul-19 | EH335 | YW19VVH | Aug-19 |
| EH314 | YW19VPF | Jul-19 | EH325 | YW19VPU | Jul-19 | EH336 | YW19VVJ | Aug-19 |
| EH315 | YW19VPG | Jul-19 | EH326 | YW19VPV | Jul-19 | EH337 | YW19VVK | Aug-19 |
| EH316 | YW19VPJ | Jul-19 | EH327 | YW19VPX | Jul 19 | EH338 | YW19VVL | Aug-19 |
| EH317 | YW19VPK | Jul-19 | EH328 | YW19VVA | Aug-19 | EH339 | YW19VVM | Aug-19 |
| EH318 | YW19VPL | Jul-19 | EH329 | YW19VVB | Aug-19 | EH340 | YW19VVN | Aug-19 |
| EH319 | YW19VPM | Jul-19 | EH330 | YW19VVC | Aug-19 | EH341 | YW19VVO | Aug-19 |
| EH320 | YW19VPN | Jul-19 | EH331 | YW19VVD | Aug-19 | EH342 | YW19VVP | Aug-19 |
| EH321 | YW19VPO | Jul-19 | EH332 | YW19VVE | Aug-19 | EH343 | YW19VVR | Aug-19 |

**EHV1 – EHV16** **Volvo B5TL** **AD Enviro 400 MMC**

| | | | | | | | | |
|---|---|---|---|---|---|---|---|---|
| EHV 1 | BK15AZR | Jun-15 | EHV 7 | BL15HBO | Jun-15 | EHV13 | BL15HCA | Jun-15 |
| EHV 2 | BK15AZT | Jun-15 | EHV 8 | BL15HBP | Jun-15 | EHV14 | BL15HCC | Jun-15 |
| EHV 3 | BJ15TWL | Jun-15 | EHV 9 | BL15HBU | Jun-15 | EHV15 | BL15HCD | Jun-15 |
| EHV 4 | BL15HBK | Jun-15 | EHV10 | BL15HBX | Jun-15 | EHV16 | BL15HBN | Jun-15 |
| EHV 5 | BJ15TWP | Jun-15 | EHV11 | BL15HBY | Jun-15 | | | |
| EHV 6 | BL15HBJ | Jun-15 | EHV12 | BL15HBZ | Jun-15 | | | |

# Metroline

**BDE2613 – BDE2649** **BYD D8UR DD** **AD Enviro 400 City EV**

| | | | | | | | | |
|---|---|---|---|---|---|---|---|---|
| BDE2613 | LJ19CTX | Nov-19 | BDE2626 | LJ19CUY | Jun-19 | BDE2639 | LJ19CVO | Jul-19 |
| BDE2614 | LJ19CTY | May-19 | BDE2627 | LJ19CVA | Jul-19 | BDE2640 | LJ19CVP | Oct-19 |
| BDE2615 | LJ19CTZ | May-19 | BDE2628 | LJ19CVB | Jul-19 | BDE2641 | LJ19CVR | Sep-19 |
| BDE2616 | LJ19CUA | May-19 | BDE2629 | LJ19CVC | Jun-19 | BDE2642 | LJ19CVS | Sep-19 |
| BDE2617 | LJ19CUC | May-19 | BDE2630 | LJ19CVD | Jun-19 | BDE2643 | LJ19CVT | Aug-19 |
| BDE2618 | LJ19CUG | May-19 | BDE2631 | LJ19CVE | Aug-19 | BDE2644 | LJ19CVU | Sep-19 |
| BDE2619 | LJ19CUH | Jun-19 | BDE2632 | LJ19CVF | Jul-19 | BDE2645 | LJ19CVV | Aug-19 |
| BDE2620 | LJ19CUK | Jun-19 | BDE2633 | LJ19CVG | Jul-19 | BDE2646 | LJ19CVW | Sep-19 |
| BDE2621 | LJ19CUO | Jun-19 | BDE2634 | LJ19CVH | Jul-19 | BDE2647 | LJ19CVX | Sep-19 |
| BDE2622 | LJ19CUU | Jun-19 | BDE2635 | LJ19CVK | Aug-19 | BDE2648 | LJ19CVY | Oct-19 |
| BDE2623 | LJ19CUV | Jul-19 | BDE2636 | LJ19CVL | Jul-19 | BDE2649 | LJ19CVZ | Oct-19 |
| BDE2624 | LJ19CUW | Jun-19 | BDE2637 | LJ19CVM | Jul-19 | | | |
| BDE2625 | LJ19CUX | Jun-19 | BDE2638 | LJ19CVN | Oct-19 | | | |

**BDE2752 – BDE2768** **BYD D8UR DD** **AD Enviro 400 City EV**

| | | | | | | | | |
|---|---|---|---|---|---|---|---|---|
| BDE2752 | LG22AXF | Jul-22 | BDE2758 | LG22AXO | Aug-22 | BDE2764 | LG22AXV | Aug-22 |
| BDE2753 | LG22AXH | Jul-22 | BDE2759 | LG22AXP | Aug-22 | BDE2765 | LG22AXW | Aug-22 |
| BDE2754 | LG22AXJ | Jul-22 | BDE2760 | LG22AXR | Aug-22 | BDE2766 | LG22AXX | Aug-22 |
| BDE2755 | LG22AXK | Jul-22 | BDE2761 | LG22AXS | Aug-22 | BDE2767 | LG22AXY | Aug-22 |
| BDE2756 | LG22AXM | Jul-22 | BDE2762 | LG22AXT | Aug-22 | BDE2768 | LG22AXZ | Aug-22 |
| BDE2757 | LG22AXN | Aug-22 | BDE2763 | LG22AXU | Aug-22 | | | |

**TEH2072 – TEH2087** **AD E40H** **AD Enviro 400 MMC**

| | | | | | | | | |
|---|---|---|---|---|---|---|---|---|
| TEH2072 | LK15CWA | Feb-15 | TEH2078 | LK15CSV | Mar-15 | TEH2084 | LK15CUA | Mar-15 |
| TEH2073 | LK15CWC | Feb-15 | TEH2079 | LK15CSX | Mar-15 | TEH2085 | LK15CUC | Mar-15 |
| TEH2074 | LK15CRZ | Mar-15 | TEH2080 | LK15CSY | Mar-15 | TEH2086 | LK15CUG | Mar-15 |
| TEH2075 | LK15CSF | Mar-15 | TEH2081 | LK15CSZ | Mar-15 | TEH2087 | LK15CUH | Mar-15 |
| TEH2076 | LK15CSO | Mar-15 | TEH2082 | LK15CTE | Mar-15 | | | |
| TEH2077 | LK15CSU | Mar-15 | TEH2083 | LK15CTF | Mar-15 | | | |

# RATP London

**ADH45258 – ADH45261** **AD E40H** **AD Enviro 400 MMC**

| | | | | | | | | |
|---|---|---|---|---|---|---|---|---|
| ADH45258 | YY67UUO | Feb-18 | ADH45260 | YY67UUR | Feb-18 | ADH45261 | YY67UUS | Feb-18 |
| ADH45259 | YY67UUP | Feb-18 | | | | | | |

**ADH45278 – ADH45297** **AD E40H** **AD Enviro 400 MMC**

| | | | | | | | | |
|---|---|---|---|---|---|---|---|---|
| ADH45278 | YX68UNH | Sep-18 | ADH45281 | YX68UNL | Sep-18 | ADH45284 | YX68UNP | Sep-18 |
| ADH45279 | YX68UNJ | Sep-18 | ADH45282 | YX68UNM | Sep-18 | ADH45285 | YX68UNS | Sep-18 |
| ADH45280 | YX68UNK | Sep-18 | ADH45283 | YX68UNN | Sep-18 | ADH45286 | YX68UNU | Sep-18 |

| | | | | | | | | |
|---|---|---|---|---|---|---|---|---|
| ADH45287 | YX68UNV | Sep-18 | ADH45291 | YX68UOL | Oct-18 | ADH45295 | YX68UOP | Oct-18 |
| ADH45288 | YX68UNW | Sep-18 | ADH45292 | YX68UOM | Oct-18 | ADH45296 | YX68UOR | Oct-18 |
| ADH45289 | YX68UOJ | Oct-18 | ADH45293 | YX68UON | Oct-18 | ADH45297 | YX68UOS | Oct-18 |
| ADH45290 | YX68UOK | Oct-18 | ADH45294 | YX68UOO | Oct-18 | | | |

**BCE47001 – BCE47021** **BYD D8UR DD** **AD Enviro 400EV City**

| | | | | | | | | |
|---|---|---|---|---|---|---|---|---|
| BCE47001 | LB69JNJ | Dec-19 | BCE47011 | LB69JOH | Jan-20 | BCE47021 | LB69JPY | Jan-20 |
| BCE47002 | LB69JNK | Dec-19 | BCE47012 | LB69JOJ | Jan-20 | BCE47022 | LB69LRO | Jan-20 |
| BCE47003 | LB69JNL | Dec-19 | BCE47013 | LB69JOU | Jan-20 | BCE47023 | LB69JRU | Jan-20 |
| BCE47004 | LB69JNN | Dec-19 | BCE47014 | LB69JOV | Jan-20 | BCE47024 | LB69JRV | Jan-20 |
| BCE47005 | LB69JNO | Dec-19 | BCE47015 | LB69JPF | Jan-20 | BCE47025 | LB69JRX | Jan-20 |
| BCE47006 | LB69JNU | Dec-19 | BCE47016 | LB69JPJ | Jan-20 | BCE47026 | LB69JRZ | Jan-20 |
| BCE47007 | LB69LNV | Dec-19 | BCE47017 | LB69JPO | Jan-20 | BCE47027 | LB69JSU | Jan-20 |
| BCE47008 | LB69LNX | Dec-19 | BCE47018 | LB69JPU | Jan-20 | BCE47028 | LB69JSV | Jan-20 |
| BCE47009 | LB69JNZ | Jan-20 | BCE47019 | LB69JPV | Jan-20 | BCE47029 | LB69JSX | Jan-20 |
| BCE47010 | LB69JOA | Jan-20 | BCE47020 | LB69JPX | Jan-20 | | | |

**BCE47030 – BCE47110** **BYD D8UR DD** **AD Enviro 400EV City**

| | | | | | | | | |
|---|---|---|---|---|---|---|---|---|
| BCE47030 | LG71DVM | Jun-21 | BCE47057 | LG71DXV | Nov-21 | BCE47084 | LE21FTF | Aug-21 |
| BCE47031 | LE21FRV | Jul-21 | BCE47058 | LG71DXW | Nov-21 | BCE47085 | LE21FTJ | Aug-21 |
| BCE47032 | LE21FRX | Jul-21 | BCE47059 | LG71DXX | Nov-21 | BCE47086 | LE21FTK | Aug-21 |
| BCE47033 | LE21FRZ | Jul-21 | BCE47060 | LG71DXY | Nov-21 | BCE47087 | LG71DWA | Oct-21 |
| BCE47034 | LE21FSA | Jul-21 | BCE47061 | LG71DXZ | Nov-21 | BCE47088 | LG71DWC | Oct-21 |
| BCE47035 | LG71DVN | Sep-21 | BCE47062 | LG71DYA | Nov-21 | BCE47089 | LG71DWD | Oct-21 |
| BCE47036 | LE21FSD | Aug-21 | BCE47063 | LG71DYB | Nov-21 | BCE47090 | LG71DWE | Oct-21 |
| BCE47037 | LE21FSF | Aug-21 | BCE47064 | LG71DYC | Nov-21 | BCE47091 | LG71DWF | Oct-21 |
| BCE47038 | LE21FSG | Aug-21 | BCE47065 | LG71DYD | Nov-21 | BCE47092 | LG71DWJ | Oct-21 |
| BCE47039 | LE21FSJ | Aug-21 | BCE47066 | LG71DYF | Nov-21 | BCE47093 | LG71DWK | Sep-21 |
| BCE47040 | LE21FSK | Aug-21 | BCE47067 | LG71DYH | Nov-21 | BCE47094 | LG71DWL | Oct-21 |
| BCE47041 | LG71DVO | Sep-21 | BCE47068 | LG71DYJ | Nov-21 | BCE47095 | LG71DWM | Sep-21 |
| BCE47042 | LG71DVP | Sep-21 | BCE47069 | LG71DYM | Nov-21 | BCE47096 | LG71DWN | Oct-21 |
| BCE47043 | LG71DVR | Sep-21 | BCE47070 | LG71DYN | Nov-21 | BCE47097 | LG71DWO | Oct-21 |
| BCE47044 | LE21FSP | Aug-21 | BCE47071 | LG71DYO | Nov-21 | BCE47098 | LG71DWP | Sep-21 |
| BCE47045 | LG71DVT | Sep-21 | BCE47072 | LG71DYP | Nov-21 | BCE47099 | LG71DWU | Oct-21 |
| BCE47046 | LG71DVU | Oct-21 | BCE47073 | LG71DYT | Nov-21 | BCE47100 | LG71DUU | Oct-21 |
| BCE47047 | LG71DVV | Sep-21 | BCE47074 | LG71DYU | Nov-21 | BCE47101 | LG71DUV | Oct-21 |
| BCE47048 | LG71DVW | Oct-21 | BCE47075 | LG71DYV | Nov-21 | BCE47102 | LG71DUY | Oct-21 |
| BCE47049 | LG71DVX | Oct-21 | BCE47076 | LG71DYW | Nov-21 | BCE47103 | LG71DVA | Oct-21 |
| BCE47050 | LG71DVY | Oct-21 | BCE47077 | LG71DYX | Nov-21 | BCE47104 | LG71DVB | Oct-21 |
| BCE47051 | LG71DVZ | Oct-21 | BCE47078 | LG71DYY | Nov-21 | BCE47105 | LG71DVC | Oct-21 |
| BCE47052 | LG71DSX | Oct-21 | BCE47079 | LG71DZA | Nov-21 | BCE47106 | LG71DVF | Oct-21 |
| BCE47053 | LG71DSY | Oct-21 | BCE47080 | LG71DZB | Nov-21 | BCE47107 | LG71DVH | Oct-21 |
| BCE47054 | LG71DXS | Nov-21 | BCE47081 | LG71DZC | Nov-21 | BCE47108 | LG71DVJ | Oct-21 |
| BCE47055 | LG71DXT | Nov-21 | BCE47082 | LG71DZE | Nov-21 | BCE47109 | LG71DVK | Oct-21 |
| BCE47056 | LG71DXU | Nov-21 | BCE47083 | LG71DZF | Nov-21 | BCE47110 | LG71DVL | Oct-21 |

**BCE47111 – BCE47137** **BYD D8UR DD** **AD Enviro 400EV City**

| | | | | | | | | |
|---|---|---|---|---|---|---|---|---|
| BCE47111 | LG22ATX | Mar-22 | BCE47120 | LG22AUK | Mar-22 | BCE47129 | LG22AUV | May-22 |
| BCE47112 | LG22ATY | Mar-22 | BCE47121 | LG22AUL | Mar-22 | BCE47130 | LG22AUW | May-22 |
| BCE47113 | LG22ATZ | Mar-22 | BCE47122 | LG22AUM | Mar-22 | BCE47131 | LG22AUX | May-22 |
| BCE47114 | LG22AUA | Mar-22 | BCE47123 | LG22AUN | Mar-22 | BCE47132 | LG22AUY | May-22 |
| BCE47115 | LG22AUC | Mar-22 | BCE47124 | LG22AUO | Mar-22 | BCE47133 | LG22AVB | May-22 |
| BCE47116 | LG22AUE | Mar-22 | BCE47125 | LG22AUP | Mar-22 | BCE47134 | LG22AVC | May-22 |
| BCE47117 | LG22AUF | Mar-22 | BCE47126 | LG22AUR | May-22 | BCE47135 | LG22AVD | May-22 |
| BCE47118 | LG22AUH | Mar-22 | BCE47127 | LG22AUT | May-22 | BCE47136 | LG22AVE | May-22 |
| BCE47119 | LG22AUJ | Mar-22 | BCE47128 | LG22AUU | May-22 | BCE47137 | LG22AVF | May-22 |

**BCE47138 – BCE47156** **BYD D8UR DD** **AD Enviro 400EV City**

| | | | | | | | | |
|---|---|---|---|---|---|---|---|---|
| BCE47138 | LG71DWV | Feb-22 | BCE47145 | LG71DXC | Feb-22 | BCE47152 | LG71DXL | Feb-22 |
| BCE47139 | LG71DWW | Feb-22 | BCE47146 | LG71DXD | Feb-22 | BCE47153 | LG71DXM | Feb-22 |
| BCE47140 | LG71DWX | Feb-22 | BCE47147 | LG71DXE | Feb-22 | BCE47154 | LG71DXO | Feb-22 |
| BCE47141 | LG71DWY | Feb-22 | BCE47148 | LG71DXF | Feb-22 | BCE47155 | LG71DXP | Feb-22 |
| BCE47142 | LG71DWZ | Feb-22 | BCE47149 | LG71DXH | Feb-22 | BCE47156 | LG71DXR | Feb-22 |
| BCE47143 | LG71DXA | Feb-22 | BCE47150 | LG71DXJ | Feb-22 | | | |
| BCE47144 | LG71DXB | Feb-22 | BCE47151 | LG71DXK | Feb-22 | | | |

**BCE47157 – BCE47177** **BYD D8UR DD** **AD Enviro 400EV City**

| | | | | | | | | |
|---|---|---|---|---|---|---|---|---|
| BCE47157 | LG72EEA | Dec-22 | BCE47164 | LD72UFZ | Dec-22 | BCE47171 | LD72UGJ | Dec-22 |
| BCE47158 | LG72EEB | Dec-22 | BCE47165 | LD72UGA | Dec-22 | BCE47172 | LD72UGK | Dec-22 |
| BCE47159 | LG72EEF | Dec-22 | BCE47166 | LD72UGB | Dec-22 | BCE47173 | LD72UGL | Dec-22 |
| BCE47160 | LD72UFV | Dec-22 | BCE47167 | LD72UGC | Dec-22 | BCE47174 | LD72UGM | Dec-22 |
| BCE47161 | LD72UFW | Dec-22 | BCE47168 | LD72UGE | Dec-22 | BCE47175 | LD72UGN | Dec-22 |
| BCE47162 | LD72UFX | Dec-22 | BCE47169 | LD72UGF | Dec-22 | BCE47176 | LD72UGO | Dec-22 |
| BCE47163 | LD72UFY | Dec-22 | BCE47170 | LD72UGG | Dec-22 | BCE47177 | LD72UGP | Dec-22 |

## Stagecoach London

**10301 – 10307** **AD E40D** **AD Enviro 400 MMC**

| | | | | | | | | |
|---|---|---|---|---|---|---|---|---|
| 10301 | YY15OYS | Jun-15 | 10304 | YY15OYV | Jun-15 | 10306 | YY15OYX | Jul-15 |
| 10302 | YY15OYT | Jun-15 | 10305 | YY15OYW | Jul-15 | 10307 | YY15OYZ | Jul-15 |
| 10303 | YY15OYU | Jun-15 | | | | | | |

**10308 – 10350** **AD E40D** **AD Enviro 400 MMC**

| | | | | | | | | |
|---|---|---|---|---|---|---|---|---|
| 10308 | SN16OJM | Mar-16 | 10312 | SN16OJS | Mar-16 | 10316 | SN16OJW | Apr-16 |
| 10309 | SN16OJO | Apr-16 | 10313 | SN16OJT | Mar-16 | 10317 | SN16OJX | Apr-16 |
| 10310 | SN16OJP | Mar-16 | 10314 | SN16OJU | Apr-16 | 10318 | SN16OJY | Apr-16 |
| 10311 | SN16OJR | Mar-16 | 10315 | SN16OJV | Mar-16 | 10319 | SN16OJZ | Apr-16 |

| 10320 | SN16OKA | Apr-16 | 10331 | SN16OKO | Mar-16 | 10342 | SN16OLC | Apr-16 |
|---|---|---|---|---|---|---|---|---|
| 10321 | SN16OKB | Apr-16 | 10332 | SN16OKP | Mar-16 | 10343 | SN16OLG | Apr-16 |
| 10322 | SN16OKC | Apr-16 | 10333 | SN16OKR | Apr-16 | 10344 | SN16OLH | Apr-16 |
| 10323 | SN16OKD | Apr-16 | 10334 | SN16OKS | Apr-16 | 10345 | SN16OLJ | Apr-16 |
| 10324 | SN16OKF | Apr-16 | 10335 | SN16OKT | Apr-16 | 10346 | SN16OLK | Apr-16 |
| 10325 | SN16OKG | Apr-16 | 10336 | SN16OKU | Apr-16 | 10347 | SN16OLO | Apr-16 |
| 10326 | SN16OKH | Mar-16 | 10337 | SN16OKV | Apr-16 | 10348 | YX66WCT | Sep-16 |
| 10327 | SN16OKJ | Mar-16 | 10338 | SN16OKW | Apr-16 | 10349 | YX66WCU | Sep-16 |
| 10328 | SN16OKK | Mar-16 | 10339 | SN16OKX | Apr-16 | 10350 | YX66WCR | Sep-16 |
| 10329 | SN16OKL | Mar-16 | 10340 | SN16OKZ | Apr-16 | | | |
| 10330 | SN16OKM | Mar-16 | 10341 | SN16OLB | Apr-16 | | | |

**11001 – 11016** **AD E40D Smart hybrid** **AD Enviro 400 MMC**

| 11001 | YY18TKZ | Aug-18 | 11007 | YY18TLV | Aug-18 | 11013 | YY18TMX | Aug-18 |
|---|---|---|---|---|---|---|---|---|
| 11002 | YY18TLF | Aug-18 | 11008 | YY18TLX | Aug-18 | 11014 | YY18TMZ | Aug-18 |
| 11003 | YY18TLJ | Aug-18 | 11009 | YY18TLZ | Aug-18 | 11015 | YY18TNE | Aug-18 |
| 11004 | YY18TLK | Aug-18 | 11010 | YY18TMO | Aug-18 | 11016 | YY18TNF | Aug-18 |
| 11005 | YY18TLN | Aug-18 | 11011 | YY18TMU | Aug-18 | | | |
| 11006 | YY18TLU | Aug-18 | 11012 | YY18TMV | Aug-18 | | | |

**11017 – 11032** **AD E40D Smart hybrid** **AD Enviro 400 MMC**

| 11017 | YX68UKA | Sep-18 | 11023 | YX68UKH | Sep-18 | 11029 | YX68UKO | Sep-18 |
|---|---|---|---|---|---|---|---|---|
| 11018 | YX68UKB | Sep-18 | 11024 | YX68UKJ | Sep-18 | 11030 | YX68UKP | Sep-18 |
| 11019 | YX68UKD | Sep-18 | 11025 | YX68UKK | Sep-18 | 11031 | YX68UKR | Sep-18 |
| 11020 | YX68UKE | Sep-18 | 11026 | YX68UKL | Sep-18 | 11032 | YX68UKS | Sep-18 |
| 11021 | YX68UKF | Sep-18 | 11027 | YX68UKM | Sep-18 | | | |
| 11022 | YX68UKG | Sep-18 | 11028 | YX68UKN | Sep-18 | | | |

**11033 – 11043** **AD E40D Smart hybrid** **AD Enviro 400 MMC**

| 11033 | SN18KTX | Jun-18 | 11037 | SN18KUD | Jun-18 | 11041 | SN18KUH | Jul-18 |
|---|---|---|---|---|---|---|---|---|
| 11034 | SN18KUA | Jun-18 | 11038 | SN18KUE | Jun-18 | 11042 | SN18KUJ | Jul-18 |
| 11035 | SN18KUB | Jun-18 | 11039 | SN18KUF | Jun-18 | 11043 | SN18KUK | Jul-18 |
| 11036 | SN18KUC | Jun-18 | 11040 | SN18KUG | Jun-18 | | | |

**11044 – 11054** **AD E40D Smart hybrid** **AD Enviro 400 MMC**

| 11044 | YY18TGF | Jul-18 | 11048 | YY18TGO | Jul-18 | 11052 | YY18TGZ | Jul-18 |
|---|---|---|---|---|---|---|---|---|
| 11045 | YY18TGJ | Jul-18 | 11049 | YY18TGU | Jul-18 | 11053 | YY18THF | Jul-18 |
| 11046 | YY18TGK | Jul-18 | 11050 | YY18TGV | Jul-18 | 11054 | YY18THG | Jul-18 |
| 11047 | YY18TGN | Jul-18 | 11051 | YY18TGX | Jul-18 | | | |

**11055 – 11074** **AD E40D Smart hybrid** **AD Enviro 400 MMC**

| | | | | | | | | |
|---|---|---|---|---|---|---|---|---|
| 11055 | YX68UMU | Sep-18 | 11062 | YX68UNF | Sep-18 | 11069 | YX68UTM | Nov-18 |
| 11056 | YX68UMV | Sep-18 | 11063 | YX68UNG | Sep-18 | 11070 | YX68UTN | Nov-18 |
| 11057 | YX68UMW | Sep-18 | 11064 | YX68UTG | Nov-18 | 11071 | YX68UTO | Nov-18 |
| 11058 | YX68UMY | Sep-18 | 11065 | YX68UTH | Nov-18 | 11072 | YX68UTP | Nov-18 |
| 11059 | YX68UMZ | Sep-18 | 11066 | YX68UTJ | Nov-18 | 11073 | YX68UTR | Nov-18 |
| 11060 | YX68UNB | Sep-18 | 11067 | YX68UTK | Nov-18 | 11074 | YX68UTT | Nov-18 |
| 11061 | YX68UNE | Sep-18 | 11068 | YX68UTL | Nov-18 | | | |

**11075 – 11081** **AD E40D Smart hybrid** **AD Enviro 400 MMC**

| | | | | | | | | |
|---|---|---|---|---|---|---|---|---|
| 11075 | YX19OMA | May-19 | 11078 | YX19OME | May-19 | 11080 | YX19OMG | May-19 |
| 11076 | YX19OMC | May-19 | 11079 | YX19OMF | May-19 | 11081 | YX19OMH | May-19 |
| 11077 | YX19OMD | May-19 | | | | | | |

**11301 – 11335** **AD E40D Smart hybrid** **AD Enviro 400 MMC**

| | | | | | | | | |
|---|---|---|---|---|---|---|---|---|
| 11301 | SO68HDJ | Feb-19 | 11313 | SK19ELH | Mar-19 | 11325 | YW68OZO | Jan-19 |
| 11302 | SO68HDK | Feb-19 | 11314 | SK19ELJ | Mar-19 | 11326 | YW68OZP | Feb-19 |
| 11303 | SO68HDL | Feb-19 | 11315 | SK19ELO | Mar-19 | 11327 | YW68OZR | Feb-19 |
| 11304 | SO68HDN | Feb-19 | 11316 | SK19ELU | Mar-19 | 11328 | YW68OZS | Feb-19 |
| 11305 | SO68HDU | Feb-19 | 11317 | YW68PCV | Jan-19 | 11329 | YW68OZT | Feb-19 |
| 11306 | SO68HDV | Feb-19 | 11318 | YW68PCU | Jan-19 | 11330 | YW68OZU | Feb-19 |
| 11307 | SO68HDX | Feb-19 | 11319 | YW68PCO | Jan-19 | 11331 | YW68OZV | Feb-19 |
| 11308 | SO68HDY | Feb-19 | 11320 | YW68PCF | Jan-19 | 11332 | YW68OZX | Feb-19 |
| 11309 | SK19EKX | Mar-19 | 11321 | YW68PBZ | Jan-19 | 11333 | YW68PAO | Feb-19 |
| 11310 | SK19EKY | Mar-19 | 11322 | YW68OZL | Jan-19 | 11334 | YW68PBF | Feb-19 |
| 11311 | SK19EKZ | Mar-19 | 11323 | YW68OZM | Jan-19 | 11335 | YW68PBO | Feb-19 |
| 11312 | SK19ELC | Mar-19 | 11324 | YW68OZN | Jan-19 | | | |

**11341 – 11399** **AD E40D Smart hybrid** **AD Enviro 400 MMC**

| | | | | | | | | |
|---|---|---|---|---|---|---|---|---|
| 11341 | SK20AXT | Apr-20 | 11350 | SK20AYC | Apr-20 | 11359 | SK20AYO | Apr-20 |
| 11342 | SK20AXU | Apr-20 | 11351 | SK20AYD | Apr-20 | 11360 | SK20AYP | Apr-20 |
| 11343 | SK20AXV | Apr-20 | 11352 | SK20AYF | Apr-20 | 11361 | SK20AYS | Apr-20 |
| 11344 | SK20AXW | Apr-20 | 11353 | SK20AYG | Apr-20 | 11362 | SK20AYT | Apr-20 |
| 11345 | SK20AXX | Apr-20 | 11354 | SK20AYH | Apr-20 | 11363 | SK20AYU | Apr-20 |
| 11346 | SK20AXY | Apr-20 | 11355 | SK20AYJ | Apr-20 | 11364 | SK20AYV | Apr-20 |
| 11347 | SK20AXZ | Apr-20 | 11356 | SK20AYL | Apr-20 | 11365 | SK20AYW | Apr-20 |
| 11348 | SK20AYA | Apr-20 | 11357 | SK20AYM | Apr-20 | 11366 | SK20AYX | Apr-20 |
| 11349 | SK20AYB | Apr-20 | 11358 | SK20AYN | Apr-20 | 11367 | SK20AYY | Apr-20 |

| | | | | | | | | |
|---|---|---|---|---|---|---|---|---|
| 11368 | SK20AYZ | Apr-20 | 11379 | SK20BBN | Jul-20 | 11390 | SK20BCX | Aug-20 |
| 11369 | SK20AZA | Apr-20 | 11380 | SK20BBO | Jul-20 | 11391 | SK20BCY | Aug-20 |
| 11370 | SK20AZB | May-20 | 11381 | SK20BBU | Jul-20 | 11392 | SK20BCZ | Aug-20 |
| 11371 | SK20AZC | May-20 | 11382 | SK20BBV | Jul-20 | 11393 | SK20BDE | Aug-20 |
| 11372 | SK20AZD | May-20 | 11383 | SK20BBX | Jul-20 | 11394 | SK20BDF | Aug-20 |
| 11373 | SK20AZF | May-20 | 11384 | SK20BBZ | Aug-20 | 11395 | SK20BDO | Aug-20 |
| 11374 | SK20AZG | May-20 | 11385 | SK20BCE | Aug-20 | 11396 | SK20BDU | Aug-20 |
| 11375 | SK20AZJ | May-20 | 11386 | SK20BCF | Aug-20 | 11397 | SK20BDV | Aug-20 |
| 11376 | SK20BBE | Jul-20 | 11387 | SK20BCO | Aug-20 | 11398 | SK20BDX | Aug-20 |
| 11377 | SK20BBF | Jul-20 | 11388 | SK20BCU | Aug-20 | 11399 | SK20BDY | Aug-20 |
| 11378 | SK20BBJ | Jul-20 | 11389 | SK20BCV | Aug-20 | | | |

**12365 – 12402** **AD E40H** **AD Enviro 400 MMC**

| | | | | | | | | |
|---|---|---|---|---|---|---|---|---|
| 12365 | YX16OGD | Jun-16 | 12378 | YX16OGS | Jun-16 | 12391 | YX16OHG | Jun-16 |
| 12366 | YX16OGE | Jul-16 | 12379 | YX16OGT | Jun-16 | 12392 | YX16OHH | Jul-16 |
| 12367 | YX16OGF | Jun-16 | 12380 | YX16OGU | Jun-16 | 12393 | YX16OHJ | Jul-16 |
| 12368 | YX16OGG | Jul-16 | 12381 | YX16OGV | Jul-16 | 12394 | YX16OHK | Jul-16 |
| 12369 | YX16OGH | Jul-16 | 12382 | YX16OGW | Jun-16 | 12395 | YX16OHL | Jul-16 |
| 12370 | YX16OGJ | Jun-16 | 12383 | YX16OGY | Jul-16 | 12396 | YX16OHN | Jul-16 |
| 12371 | YX16OGK | Jun-16 | 12384 | YX16OGZ | Jul-16 | 12397 | YX16OHO | Jul-16 |
| 12372 | YX16OGL | Jun-16 | 12385 | YX16OHA | Jun-16 | 12398 | YX16OHP | Jul-16 |
| 12373 | YX16OGM | Jun-16 | 12386 | YX16OHB | Jul-16 | 12399 | YX16OHR | Jul-16 |
| 12374 | YX16OGN | Jun-16 | 12387 | YX16OHC | Jun-16 | 12400 | YX16OHS | Jul-16 |
| 12375 | YX16OGO | Jun-16 | 12388 | YX16OHD | Jun-16 | 12401 | YX66WCP | Sep-16 |
| 12376 | YX16OGP | Jun-16 | 12389 | YX16OHE | Jul-16 | 12402 | YX66WAU | Oct-16 |
| 12377 | YX16OGR | Jun-16 | 12390 | YX16OHF | Jul-16 | | | |

**12403 – 12425** **AD E40H** **AD Enviro 400 MMC**

| | | | | | | | | |
|---|---|---|---|---|---|---|---|---|
| 12403 | YY66PHA | Jan-17 | 12411 | YY66PHX | Feb-17 | 12419 | YY66PKC | Feb-17 |
| 12404 | YY66PHF | Jan-17 | 12412 | YY66PHZ | Feb-17 | 12420 | YY66PKD | Feb-17 |
| 12405 | YY66PFJ | Jan-17 | 12413 | YY66PJJ | Feb-17 | 12421 | YY66PKE | Feb-17 |
| 12406 | YY66PHK | Jan-17 | 12414 | YY66PJO | Feb-17 | 12422 | YY66PKF | Feb-17 |
| 12407 | YY66PHN | Jan-17 | 12415 | YY66PJU | Feb-17 | 12423 | YY66PXT | Feb-17 |
| 12408 | YY66PHO | Jan-17 | 12416 | YY66PJV | Feb-17 | 12424 | YY66PXU | Feb-17 |
| 12409 | YY66PHU | Jan-17 | 12417 | YY66PJX | Feb-17 | 12425 | YY66PXV | Feb-17 |
| 12410 | YY66PHV | Feb-17 | 12418 | YY66PKA | Feb-17 | | | |

**12426 – 12432** **AD E40H** **AD Enviro 400 MMC**

| | | | | | | | | |
|---|---|---|---|---|---|---|---|---|
| 12426 | YX67VBC | Sep-17 | 12429 | YX67VBF | Sep-17 | 12431 | YX67VBJ | Sep-17 |
| 12427 | YX67VBD | Sep-17 | 12430 | YX67VBG | Sep-17 | 12432 | YX67VBK | Sep-17 |
| 12428 | YX67VBE | Sep-17 | | | | | | |

**12433 – 12451** **AD E40H** **AD Enviro 400 MMC**

| | | | | | | | | |
|---|---|---|---|---|---|---|---|---|
| 12433 | SN67XDW | Feb-18 | 12440 | SN67XEE | Feb-18 | 12447 | SN67XEM | Feb-18 |
| 12434 | SN67XDX | Feb-18 | 12441 | SN67XEF | Feb-18 | 12448 | SN67XEO | Feb-18 |
| 12435 | SN67XDY | Feb-18 | 12442 | SN67XEG | Feb-18 | 12449 | SN67XEP | Feb-18 |
| 12436 | SN67XDZ | Feb-18 | 12443 | SN67XEH | Feb-18 | 12450 | SN67XER | Feb-18 |
| 12437 | SN67XEB | Feb-18 | 12444 | SN67XEJ | Feb-18 | 12451 | SN67XES | Feb-18 |
| 12438 | SN67XEC | Feb-18 | 12445 | SN67XEK | Feb-18 | | | |
| 12439 | SN67XED | Feb-18 | 12446 | SN67XEL | Feb-18 | | | |

**12501 – 12549** **AD E40H** **AD Enviro 400 City**

| | | | | | | | | |
|---|---|---|---|---|---|---|---|---|
| 12501 | SN16OHP | Aug-22 | 12518 | SN16OJH | Aug-22 | 12535 | SN66WRZ | Aug-22 |
| 12502 | SN16OHR | Aug-22 | 12519 | SN16OJJ | Aug-22 | 12536 | SN66WSD | Aug-22 |
| 12503 | SN16OHS | Aug-22 | 12520 | SN16OJK | Aug-22 | 12537 | SN66WSE | Aug-22 |
| 12504 | SN16OHT | Aug-22 | 12521 | SN16OJL | Aug-22 | 12538 | SN65OHP | Aug-22 |
| 12505 | SN16OHU | Aug-22 | 12522 | SN66WRE | Aug-22 | 12539 | YX19ORO | Aug-22 |
| 12506 | SN16OHV | Aug-22 | 12523 | SN66WRG | Aug-22 | 12540 | YX19ORP | Aug-22 |
| 12507 | SN16OHW | Aug-22 | 12524 | SN66WRJ | Aug-22 | 12541 | YX19ORS | Aug-22 |
| 12508 | SN16OHX | Aug-22 | 12525 | SN66WRK | Aug-22 | 12542 | YX19ORT | Aug-22 |
| 12509 | SN16OHY | Aug-22 | 12526 | SN66WRL | Aug-22 | 12543 | YX19ORU | Aug-22 |
| 12510 | SN16OHZ | Aug-22 | 12527 | SN66WRO | Aug-22 | 12544 | YX19ORV | Aug-22 |
| 12511 | SN16OJA | Aug-22 | 12528 | SN66WRP | Aug-22 | 12545 | YX19ORW | Aug-22 |
| 12512 | SN16OJB | Aug-22 | 12529 | SN66WRR | Aug-22 | 12546 | YX19ORY | Aug-22 |
| 12513 | SN16OJC | Aug-22 | 12530 | SN66WRT | Aug-22 | 12547 | YX19ORZ | Aug-22 |
| 12514 | SN16OJD | Aug-22 | 12531 | SN66WRU | Aug-22 | 12548 | YX69NLY | Aug-22 |
| 12515 | SN16OJE | Aug-22 | 12532 | SN66WRV | Aug-22 | 12549 | YX69NLZ | Aug-22 |
| 12516 | SN16OJF | Aug-22 | 12533 | SN66WRW | Aug-22 | | | |
| 12517 | SN16OJG | Aug-22 | 12534 | SN66WRX | Aug-22 | | | |

Note: 12501-12549 were acquired from CT Plus in August 2022. Dates new for these buses can be found under the CT Plus heading earlier in this Appendix.

**13061 – 13081** **Volvo B5LH** **AD Enviro 400 MMC**

| | | | | | | | | |
|---|---|---|---|---|---|---|---|---|
| 13061 | BF15KGK | May-15 | 13068 | BF15KGZ | Jun-15 | 13075 | BJ15TVZ | Jun-15 |
| 13062 | BG15KGN | May-15 | 13069 | BF15KHB | Jun-15 | 13076 | BJ15TWA | Jul-15 |
| 13063 | BF15KGP | Jun-15 | 13070 | BF15KHC | Jun-15 | 13077 | BF15KHA | Jun-15 |
| 13064 | BF15KGU | Jun-15 | 13071 | BF15KHD | Jun-15 | 13078 | BJ15TWC | Jun-15 |
| 13065 | BF15KGV | Jun-15 | 13072 | BF15KHG | Jun-15 | 13079 | BF15KGJ | Jun-15 |
| 13066 | BF15KGX | Jun-15 | 13073 | BF15KHH | Jun-15 | 13080 | BF15KGO | Jul-15 |
| 13067 | BF15KGY | Jun-15 | 13074 | BF15KHJ | Jun-15 | 13081 | BF15KHE | Jul-15 |

**13082 – 13102** **Volvo B5LH** **AD Enviro 400 MMC**

| | | | | | | | | |
|---|---|---|---|---|---|---|---|---|
| 13082 | BL65OYA | Dec-15 | 13089 | BL65OYH | Dec-15 | 13096 | BL65OYR | Jan-16 |
| 13083 | BL65OYB | Dec-15 | 13090 | BL65OYJ | Dec-15 | 13097 | BL65OYT | Jan-16 |
| 13084 | BL65OYC | Dec-15 | 13091 | BL65OYK | Dec-15 | 13098 | BL65OYU | Jan-16 |
| 13085 | BL65OYD | Dec-15 | 13092 | BL65OYM | Jan-16 | 13099 | BL65OYV | Jan-16 |
| 13086 | BL65OYE | Dec-15 | 13093 | BL65OYN | Jan-16 | 13100 | BL65OYW | Jan-16 |
| 13087 | BL65OYF | Dec-15 | 13094 | BL65OYO | Jan-16 | 13101 | BL65OYX | Jan-16 |
| 13088 | BL65OYG | Dec-15 | 13095 | BL65OYP | Jan-16 | 13102 | BL65OYY | Jan-16 |

**14101 – 14147** **BYD D8UR DD** **AD Enviro 400EV City**

| | | | | | | | | |
|---|---|---|---|---|---|---|---|---|
| 14101 | LF70YTV | Nov-20 | 14117 | LF70YUO | Mar-21 | 14133 | LF70YVK | Nov-20 |
| 14102 | LF70YTW | Nov-20 | 14118 | LF70YUR | Feb-21 | 14134 | LF70YVL | Nov-20 |
| 14103 | LF70YTX | Nov-20 | 14119 | LF70YUS | Feb-21 | 14135 | LF70YVM | Nov-20 |
| 14104 | LF70YTY | Nov-20 | 14120 | LF70YUU | Mar-21 | 14136 | LF70YVN | Nov-20 |
| 14105 | LF70YTZ | Nov-20 | 14121 | LF70YUV | Mar-21 | 14137 | LF70YVO | Nov-20 |
| 14106 | LF70YUA | Nov-20 | 14122 | LF70YUW | Mar-21 | 14138 | LF70YVP | Nov-20 |
| 14107 | LF70YUB | Dec-20 | 14123 | LF70YUX | Mar-21 | 14139 | LF70YVR | Nov-20 |
| 14108 | LF70YUC | Dec-20 | 14124 | LF70YUY | Mar-21 | 14140 | LF70YVS | Dec-20 |
| 14109 | LF70YUD | Dec-20 | 14125 | LF70YVA | Feb-21 | 14141 | LF70YVT | Dec-20 |
| 14110 | LF70YUE | Feb-21 | 14126 | LF70YVB | Mar-21 | 14142 | LF70YVU | Dec-20 |
| 14111 | LF70YUG | Feb-21 | 14127 | LF70YVC | Mar-21 | 14143 | LF70YVV | Dec-20 |
| 14112 | LF70YUH | Mar-21 | 14128 | LF70YVD | Feb-21 | 14144 | LF70YVW | Dec-20 |
| 14113 | LF70YUJ | Feb-21 | 14129 | LF70YVE | Mar-21 | 14145 | LF70YVX | Dec-20 |
| 14114 | LF70YUK | Feb-21 | 14130 | LF70YVG | Nov-20 | 14146 | LF70YVY | Dec-20 |
| 14115 | LF70YUL | Feb-21 | 14131 | LF70YVH | Nov-20 | 14147 | LF70YVZ | Dec-20 |
| 14116 | LF70YUN | Feb-21 | 14132 | LF70YVJ | Nov-20 | | | |

Note: These buses were renumbered to 84101 – 84147 in April 2023.

**14148 – 14172** **BYD D8UR DD** **AD Enviro 400EV City**

| | | | | | | | | |
|---|---|---|---|---|---|---|---|---|
| 14148 | LG71DNV | Dec-21 | 14157 | LG71DPK | Dec-21 | 14166 | LG71DRV | Dec-21 |
| 14149 | LG71DNX | Dec-21 | 14158 | LG71DPN | Dec-21 | 14167 | LG71DRX | Dec-21 |
| 14150 | LG71DNY | Dec-21 | 14159 | LG71DPO | Dec-21 | 14168 | LG71DRZ | Dec-21 |
| 14151 | LG71DOA | Dec-21 | 14160 | LG71DPU | Dec-21 | 14169 | LG71DSE | Dec-21 |
| 14152 | LG71DOH | Dec-21 | 14161 | LG71DPV | Dec-21 | 14170 | LG71DSO | Dec-21 |
| 14153 | LG71DOJ | Dec-21 | 14162 | LG71DPX | Dec-21 | 14171 | LG71DSU | Dec-21 |
| 14154 | LG71DOU | Dec-21 | 14163 | LG71DPY | Dec-21 | 14172 | LG71DSV | Dec-21 |
| 14155 | LG71DPE | Dec-21 | 14164 | LG71DPZ | Dec-21 | | | |
| 14156 | LG71DPF | Dec-21 | 14165 | LG71DRO | Dec-21 | | | |

Note: These buses were renumbered to 84148 – 84172 in April 2023.

**14173 – 14174** **BYD D8UR DD** **AD Enviro 400EV City**

| | | | | | |
|---|---|---|---|---|---|
| 14173 | LG21HZM | Aug-22 | 14174 | LG21HZN | Aug-22 |

Note: These two double-deckers were acquired from CT Plus in August 2022. The dates that these buses were new are recorded under the CT Plus heading earlier in this Appendix. 14173 and 14174 were renumbered 84173 and 84174 in April 2023.

## Sullivan Buses

**E70 – E81** **AD E40H** **AD Enviro 400 MMC**

| | | | | | | | | |
|---|---|---|---|---|---|---|---|---|
| E70 | AD17SUL | Apr-17 | E74 | JS17SUL | Apr-17 | E78 | RS17SUL | May-17 |
| E71 | AW17SUL | May-17 | E75 | PB17SUL | Apr-17 | E79 | RT17SUL | May-17 |
| E72 | BW17SUL | Apr-17 | E76 | RC17SUL | May-17 | E80 | SG17SUL | May-17 |
| E73 | JC17SUL | Apr-17 | E77 | RM17SUL | Apr-17 | E81 | WG17SUL | May-17 |

## Tower Transit

**DH38501 – DH38503** **AD E40H** **AD Enviro 400 MMC**

| | | | | | | | | |
|---|---|---|---|---|---|---|---|---|
| DH38501 | SN65ZGO | Oct-15 | DH38502 | SN65ZGP | Nov-15 | DH38503 | SN65ZGR | Nov-15 |

## Other Operators

### Reading Buses

**731 – 741** **AD E40H** **AD Enviro 400 City**

| | | | | | | | | |
|---|---|---|---|---|---|---|---|---|
| 731 | RG23BUS | Jul-23 | 735 | GL23LGO | Jul-23 | 739 | FL73WND | Feb-24 |
| 732 | GL23LDN | Jun-23 | 736 | GL23BKL | Jul-23 | 740 | FL73LGO | Feb-24 |
| 733 | GL23SLH | Jul-23 | 737 | GL23LHR | Jul-23 | 741 | RG24BUS | Mar-24 |
| 734 | GL23WND | Jul-23 | 738 | FL73LHR | Feb-24 | | | |

**757 – 795** **AD E40D** **AD Enviro 400 MMC**

| | | | | | | | | |
|---|---|---|---|---|---|---|---|---|
| 757 | YX64VRT | Oct-14 | 760 | YY15OYB | May-15 | 781 | SN66WRC | Dec-16 |
| 758 | YX64VRU | Oct-14 | 761 | YY15OYC | May-15 | 782 | SN66WRD | Dec-16 |
| 759 | YY15OYA | May-15 | 762 | YY15OYD | May-15 | 795 | SN66WLK | Oct-16 |

Note: 795 was new to ADL Limited, Falkirk as a demonstrator.

### Arriva Southern Counties

**6485 – 6498** **AD E40D** **AD Enviro 400 MMC**

| | | | | | | | | |
|---|---|---|---|---|---|---|---|---|
| 6485 | YY16YKU | Jul-16 | 6490 | YY16YLA | Jul-16 | 6495 | YY16YLF | Jul-16 |
| 6486 | YY16YKV | Jul-16 | 6491 | YY16YLB | Aug-16 | 6496 | YY16YLG | Aug-16 |
| 6487 | YY16YKW | Jul-16 | 6492 | YY16YLC | Jul-16 | 6497 | YY16YLH | Aug-16 |
| 6488 | YY16YKX | Jul-16 | 6493 | YY16YLD | Jul-16 | 6498 | YY16YLJ | Aug-16 |
| 6489 | YY16YKZ | Jul-16 | 6494 | YY16YLE | Jul-16 | | | |

## First Berkshire

**34375 – 34387** **AD E40D** **AD Enviro 400 MMC**

| | | | | | | | | |
|---|---|---|---|---|---|---|---|---|
| 34375 | SO68HFV | Feb-19 | 34380 | SO68HGA | Feb-19 | 34384 | SO68HGF | Feb-19 |
| 34376 | SO68HFW | Feb-19 | 34381 | SO68HGC | Feb-19 | 34385 | SK19EMF | Mar-19 |
| 34377 | SO68HFX | Feb-19 | 34382 | SO68HGD | Feb-19 | 34386 | SK19EMJ | Mar-19 |
| 34378 | SO68HFY | Feb-19 | 34383 | SO68HGE | Feb-19 | 34387 | SK19EMV | Mar-19 |
| 34379 | SO68HFZ | Feb-19 | | | | | | |

Note: These buses were new to First Glasgow before transferring to First Berkshire in February and March 2023.

## Carousel Buses

**608 – 614** **AD E40D** **AD Enviro 400 MMC**

| | | | | | | | | |
|---|---|---|---|---|---|---|---|---|
| 608 | RW64OXF | Sep-14 | 611 | LM64OXF | Sep-14 | 613 | JG64OXF | Sep-14 |
| 609 | PS64OXF | Sep-14 | 612 | GA64OXF | Sep-14 | 614 | GH64OXF | Sep-14 |
| 610 | PK64OXF | Sep-14 | | | | | | |

Note: These buses were new to the Oxford Bus Company before moving across to Carousel Buses, High Wycombe in 2024.

## Uno, Hatfield

**250 – 255** **AD E40D** **AD Enviro 400 City**

| | | | | | | | | |
|---|---|---|---|---|---|---|---|---|
| 250 | YX17NPZ | Jul-17 | 252 | YX17NRE | Jul-17 | 254 | YX17NRJ | Jul-17 |
| 251 | YX17NPY | Jul-17 | 253 | YX17NRF | Jul-17 | 255 | YX17NRK | Jul-17 |

**256 – 262** **AD E40D** **AD Enviro 400 MMC**

| | | | | | | | | |
|---|---|---|---|---|---|---|---|---|
| 256 | YX67VFW | Sep-17 | 259 | YX67VFS | Sep-17 | 261 | YX67VFU | Sep-17 |
| 257 | YX67VFY | Sep-17 | 260 | YX67VFT | Sep-17 | 262 | YX67VFV | Sep-17 |
| 258 | YX67VFR | Sep-17 | | | | | | |

## London Independents

| | | | | | |
|---|---|---|---|---|---|
| | SK71CKN | AD E40D | AD Enviro 400 MMC | Abbey Travel, Erith | Sep-21 |
| | SK21FHX | AD E40D | AD Enviro 400 MMC | Air Sym | Mar-21 |
| | SK72CWC | AD E40D | AD Enviro 400 MMC | BM Coaches, Hayes | Sep-22 |
| | SK72CWD | AD E40D | AD Enviro 400 MMC | BM Coaches, Hayes | Sep-22 |
| | YX67UYG | AD E40D | AD Enviro 400 MMC | Imperial Coaches | Sep-17 |
| | YX67UYH | AD E40D | AD Enviro 400 MMC | Imperial Coaches | Sep-17 |
| | YX67UYJ | AD E40D | AD Enviro 400 MMC | Imperial Coaches | Sep-17 |
| | YX67UYK | AD E40D | AD Enviro 400 MMC | Imperial Coaches | Sep-17 |
| | SK19EVP | AD E40D | AD Enviro 400 MMC | Imperial Coaches | Jan-20 |
| | SK19EVR | AD E40D | AD Enviro 400 MMC | Imperial Coaches | Jan-20 |
| | SL69XWU | AD E40D | AD Enviro 400 MMC | Imperial Coaches | Oct-20 |

| | | | | | |
|---|---|---|---|---|---|
| | SK70BVS | AD E40D | AD Enviro 400 MMC | Imperial Coaches | Oct-20 |
| | SK70BVV | AD E40D | AD Enviro 400 MMC | Imperial Coaches | Oct-20 |
| | SK21FKA | AD E40D | AD Enviro 400 MMC | Imperial Coaches | Apr-21 |
| | SK21FKB | AD E40D | AD Enviro 400 MMC | Imperial Coaches | Apr-21 |
| | SN18KLO | AD E40D | AD Enviro 400 MMC | London Travel In | Jul-18 |
| | SN18KLP | AD E40D | AD Enviro 400 MMC | London Travel In | Jul-18 |
| | SN18KSO | AD E40D | AD Enviro 400 MMC | New Punjab Coaches | Jun-18 |
| | SL69XWW | AD E40D | AD Enviro 400 MMC | New Punjab Coaches | Jan-20 |
| 191 | SK70BUH | AD E40D | AD Enviro 400 MMC | Westbus | Sep-20 |
| 192 | SK70BUJ | AD E40D | AD Enviro 400 MMC | Westbus | Sep-20 |
| 197 | SK23CUJ | AD E40D | AD Enviro 400 MMC | Westbus | May-23 |
| | YY66PXR | AD E40D | AD Enviro 400 MMC | Westway | Jan-17 |
| | YX17NUJ | AD E40D | AD Enviro 400 MMC | Westway | Mar-17 |
| | SK21FHV | AD E40D | AD Enviro 400 MMC | Westway | Jun-21 |
| | SK21FHW | AD E40D | AD Enviro 400 MMC | Westway | Jun-21 |